• • •

Tessa Takes the Challenge

• • •

Tessa Takes the Challenge

Donna Every

The ABC's of Entrepreneurship
Tessa Takes the Challenge

ISBN: 1517385342
ISBN 13: 9781517385347

This book is a work of fiction. Names, characters, places and incidents are either products of the author's imagination or are used fictitiously.

Cover design © 2015 by Simone Davis. All rights reserved.
Cover photography by Andre Williams
Model: Kim Hill

• • •

Introduction

Wait! Do not skip this introduction because it's important, trust me.

This is the first book in a series that I'm calling The ABC's of Entrepreneurship. Although I'm using the word 'Entrepreneurship', the debate about who is an entrepreneur and what is entrepreneurship continues, so don't be put off by the title. To me, what is more important is that people (especially young ones) begin to think about earning revenue by starting their own business rather than relying on a job.

I've written the book in a way that you've probably never seen in a textbook. I even hesitate to call it a textbook because it's not just for students; it's for anyone interested in starting and successfully running a business. As I was saying, I've written it differently, meaning that the first part of the book is fiction; it's a story about a student fresh out of university who couldn't find a job and decided to start her own business. I've used her story to share some of the challenges and rewards of being an entrepreneur. The second part of the book is non-fiction and gives the more textbook style information, as well as activities. The chapters in both sections have the same titles (at least most of them) so that you can relate them to each other.

I've done it like this for a number of reasons. The main one is that I want the book to be enjoyable. I remember my days of studying and the drudgery of reading through dry textbooks to extract the information I needed, so I want to spare you that.

Secondly, I know that people have different styles of learning; some are more right-brained and, therefore, are more "visual" and enjoy stories and pictures while some are left-brained and, therefore, prefer the bare facts (and often figures). So I've used both ways of presenting the information so that it will cater to the two styles.

Last of all, I've written it this way because I enjoy writing both fiction and non-fiction. You can choose if you want to read both parts of the book or just one. If you're cramming for a test or want more in-depth information, you might want to read the second part but if you want to fully understand the experience of entrepreneurship you should read the story. Both, however, will provide you with much (but not all) of the information you will need to start and run a business. I also encourage you to read online publications about successful entrepreneurs and successful businesses to encourage you and to increase your knowledge. I really hope you enjoy this book and that it inspires you to start your own business. E-mail me at donna@donnaevery.com to let me know what you think of it.

Donna Every

● ● ●
PART I

Chapter 1

• • •

Entrepreneur or Employee?

"There're just no jobs out there for me," complained Tessa, throwing down the newspaper in disgust.

"Don't give up," encouraged her fiancé, Joshua, as he slid over to her side of the couch to give her a reassuring hug.

Tessa leaned against him, absorbing the comfort he offered as she fought against giving in to despair.

"But I sacrificed and went to university and studied hard. I even got an honours degree in Business Management and I still can't find a job! What was the point?"

While Tessa vented her frustrations, ideas were beginning to turn over in Joshua's head. He could understand Tessa's frustrations; he came across many graduates like her in his business. He and a partner owned a company which sold and provided training for a popular software package designed for hotels and restaurants and he also wrote programs to enhance the software performance. He was responsible for marketing the business while his partner focused on overseeing the operations. A lot of graduates, especially with IT degrees, sent in CVs hoping to get a job with the company, even when there were no vacancies advertised, because they couldn't find jobs after leaving university.

"Going to university was not a waste of time because you've now got knowledge that you didn't have before. Maybe you should think about starting your own business," he advised her.

"Starting my own business? What would I do? I don't know anything about running a business and, anyway, I never thought about it."

"What do you mean you don't know anything about running a business? You just did a degree in Business Management."

She laughed ruefully. "Oh yeah, but that was theory. I don't have any practical experience in running a business. Anyway, when I was growing up my parents always said that I had to get a degree and find a job."

"Mine too, but that didn't stop me from starting my own business. I was lucky enough to work with a company for a couple of years before I started out on my own. It was a good experience but I saw an opportunity in the market and I took it.

"Times are changing and you're now seeing first-hand how scarce jobs are. People need to start to think about creating their own businesses and becoming entrepreneurs instead of employees. Some are forced into it when they lose their jobs or, like you, can't find a job after they have finished university and others respond to opportunities that they see in the market, like me. Entrepreneurs are very important to the economy because they create new products and services, they employ people and their businesses stimulate the economy. The ones that export and earn foreign exchange for their countries are especially important."

"I know, but the word 'entrepreneur' is kind of off-putting because I feel as if an entrepreneur is some kind of guru with amazing innovative ideas, who creates companies like Apple, Microsoft and Amazon. If that is the case, I'm definitely not an entrepreneur."

Joshua laughed. "That's not the only kind of entrepreneur and, besides, those are the exceptional ones. Let's Google 'What is an Entrepreneur?' and see what it says," he suggested, taking out his iPhone. In a few seconds a number of websites with various definitions appeared on the screen.

"Alright, the Google definition is 'A person who organizes and operates a business or businesses, taking on greater than normal financial risks in order to do so'. I don't completely agree with that because who in their right mind would take on greater than normal financial risks? Let's look at some other definitions."

"Here's another one: 'An entrepreneur is a person who organizes and manages a business undertaking, assuming the risk for the sake of profit.'[1] Again, that isn't totally true because there are also social entrepreneurs who aren't solely focused on profits."

"What's a social entrepreneur?" Tessa asked, beginning to get interested.

"A social entrepreneur is someone who sets up a business or an organization to solve social problems or bring about social change. Some of the businesses may make profits, but that is not the main purpose and some social entrepreneurship organizations are not-for-profit."

"Oh."

"This is the Wikipedia version of what entrepreneurship is. It says, 'Entrepreneurship is a process of identifying and starting a business venture, sourcing and organizing the required resources and taking both the risks and rewards associated with the venture.'[2] I like that better."

"The bottom line is that entrepreneurs are people who see an opportunity to meet a need or want and go about meeting those needs by taking some kind of financial risk, especially in uncertain times. They also have to be self-motivated, persistent and willing to persevere. Creativity and innovation are the characteristics that most people talk about but I think that scares off people because many people don't see themselves that way. "

"That's true," agreed Tessa.

"Then there are lifestyle entrepreneurs who go into business because it suits their lifestyle. They may want to be more flexible or to be their own boss, that sort of thing.

"And this week I read an article about authors as entrepreneurs," Joshua continued. "It said that some authors didn't see themselves as entrepreneurs and preferred to work with traditional publishers who take on the risk of publishing their books but because of Amazon and a number of other self-publishing platforms, a lot more authors are choosing to self-publish and they are considered to be entrepreneurs or authorpreneurs."

"I guess they do create a unique product which is their book, invest in getting it published and then they bring it to the market. That means they have to find creative ways to get people to discover and buy their book because they usually don't have a lot of money to do major marketing until they get successful. But that still doesn't make me an entrepreneur," groaned Tessa, beginning to feel down again. "I can't write books or computer programs like you and I don't have any creative or innovative ideas. What can I do?"

"The first thing you need to do is some stocktaking," advised Joshua, "and you will be surprised."

"What do you mean stocktaking? Like a shop?"

"Yes. The same way a shop shuts down for a day and the staff goes through and lists everything they have, you need to do the same thing. Tomorrow you can take my SUV and drive to a beach or park and sit down under a tree and just relax. Take your iPad and write down everything you know, everything you can do, things that you would like to buy or services that you would like but you can't get, things that you hear people complaining about, things that you are passionate about, dreams that you used to have even before you decided to go to university to do business... You get the idea?"

"Yes, yes," Tessa said eagerly, beginning to get excited for the first time. Ideas were beginning to flow into her mind already. "I knew there was a reason I'm engaged to you," she teased him, kissing his cheek.

"Then it's not just because of my SUV?"

"That too." They both laughed because they knew that things like that were not important to her and Joshua hugged her again, happy that he was able to help her begin to look at the future with hope.

Chapter 2

• • •

Closed for Stocktaking

Tessa spread her towel on the sand, sat down under a shady tree and sighed with pleasure as she looked out at the sea which, today, was a brilliant azure since there were hardly any clouds in the sky. It was low tide so the waves were breaking gently on the shore. A feeling of wellbeing came over her and she gave another satisfied sigh, glad that Joshua had given her the idea to come to the beach. There were a few tourists and locals further down the beach, enough people around for her to feel safe, but not too many to make her feel crowded. After a few minutes of relaxation she turned on her iPad, tapped on 'Notes' and opened a new one.

She typed: 'What do I know and what can I do?' Pausing, she looked at the horizon again, as if the answers were to be found there. She started to write:

Accounts and financial ratios
Marketing (in theory)
Human Resources and organizational behaviour
Operations of a company
Business documents like letters of credit, credit notes, purchase orders etc.
Word, Excel, PowerPoint, QuickBooks

She was pleased to see that she did not know "anything about running a business" as she had told Joshua. In fact, she actually knew quite a lot, although it was mostly theoretical. But at least she knew how to use QuickBooks from helping her cousin, who was an independent Accountant. She had sometimes entered data for a few of her clients to earn extra money for university.

She remembered Joshua telling her to think outside the box and not just specifically about business, so she added:

How to use Facebook, Twitter and Instagram
Fashion
How to draw and create designs
Graphic art programs

'OK, what am I passionate about?' She thought for a moment. Then she smiled to herself. She thought about how she spent a lot of her time and she realized that she was always checking out fashions. In fact, she had at one point thought about being a fashion designer but she had been dissuaded by her parents who didn't see how she could earn any real money from that unless she became famous. She was actually quite good at drawing and sketching clothes but she wasn't that keen on cutting them out and sewing them, although when she was much younger she had enjoyed sewing. She was good at creating Word Art and she also loved reading quotes and positive messages. She loved travelling and learning about other cultures.

She often created flyers and brochures since she was good at graphic art as well. In fact, whenever someone wanted a flyer done, they often called her to do it and she would do it for free because she enjoyed creating them.

She typed into her note: Passionate about fashion. Love positive messages. Enjoy creating flyers and brochures. Enjoy crafting words. Enjoy travelling and learning about other cultures.

'What can't people get here or what do I hear them complaining about?'

The first thing that popped into her mind was that just that morning her mother was complaining about how hot she was in her business suit as she left for work. Then she remembered her friends on campus complaining that they couldn't find good quality T-shirts to wear to classes.

"Hmm." She let her gaze return to the sea again even as possibilities began to fill her mind. Ideas about suits that were specifically made for hot climates and 100% cotton T-shirts that were attractive, well-made and carried positive messages for teens and younger people captivated her thoughts.

"And with the Internet I'm not limited," she said aloud. "I can create a line of clothes or inspirational T-shirts and sell them worldwide. I can use Facebook and social media to promote them."

Her index finger began to fly over the small keyboard as ideas began to flood her mind. Before she knew it she had written lines and lines of thoughts as her creative juices began to flow.

● ● ●

Joshua watched as Tessa swung his vehicle into the driveway in front of his office, braked, put the car in park and pulled up the hand brake before hopping out, leaving the motor running. He was pleased to see that she was smiling broadly as she threw herself at him and hugged him, making him stagger back a bit under the impact of the enthusiastic hug.

"Hello, wise one," she greeted him, kissing him briefly.

"Hello yourself."

He was amused and pleased by the change in her as she practically skipped around to the passenger side of his SUV.

"Am I to take it that you had a productive day?" he asked, putting the jeep in drive and letting down the handbrake.

"You got that right! It was flowing so well that I didn't even want to go anywhere to eat, so I just had the few snacks that I took with me."

"Ok, I get the hint. Let's stop for a bite on the way to your house and you can fill me in on your day."

"You better tell me about yours first because you won't get a word in once I get started."

Donna Every

He laughed and told her about the things he had accomplished as well as the frustrations he'd had during the day.

After they had ordered drinks and sandwiches at a popular sports bar, Tessa whipped out her iPad and dismissed the 'low battery' warning. Turning it towards Josh, she scrolled triumphantly through the seemingly never ending notes that she had written at the beach.

"I'm impressed. So what did you come up with?"

"I did what you suggested and took stock. First of all I asked myself 'Who am I?'"

"And who are you?" he asked teasingly. "Apart from my very sexy fiancée?" She hit him playfully on the shoulder, making a face.

"I am a creative woman who loves fashion, knows quality and loves to inspire others. I'm also a pretty good graphic artist."

"Agreed," he nodded.

"What do I know? Quite a lot about business, actually, although it's mainly theory. Accounts, Quickbooks, Word et cetera. How to create Word Art…

"Who do I know? Students, Facebook friends, you… Not a lot of people, really."

"That's OK. My network is your network," he offered generously.

"Thanks, love. Then when I thought about what I couldn't get here, I remembered not being able to find nice T-shirts to wear to campus, especially with positive messages, so I'm going to create a line of high-quality T-shirts with positive messages mainly for teenage girls and younger women. My plan is to sell them locally and internationally via the Internet and become a millionaire by thirty," she ended with a laugh.

"Then I can retire and you can support me," he teased.

"You'd be bored in a week."

"True. You said that you would target women. Not men as well?"

"No. I feel that I know what women will like more than men so I prefer to focus on women."

"OK. Sounds like a plan. But keep an open mind because you may find that there are other business ideas that may be easier to do. Bear in mind that if you're going to import T-shirts for your designs you'll have to pay duties and there'll be other costs involved."

"OK. I'll bear that in mind." Tessa smiled in anticipation as their food arrived.

Chapter 3

• • •

Market Research

"That hit the spot," Tessa said contentedly, wiping her lips on a napkin.

"Agreed. Now that you're fed and contented I have to break some news to you."

"What news?" she asked cautiously.

"Now that you've got an idea, the first thing you need to do is some market research."

Tessa groaned. "That sounds like Marketing 101," she protested. "I know that this will take off, so why do I have to do research?"

Joshua laughed sympathetically because he knew exactly what she meant. He was at the same place a few years ago but he and his partner had done their research and it was a good thing too. It saved them making a lot of mistakes. He knew that many entrepreneurs came up with an idea and just wanted to rush into it without finding out if there was really a market for their product or service. It was only the ones that were ahead of their time that created their own market but for most of them market research was a necessary "evil".

"You should know from your degree that it's important to do research. It's not a waste of time. Many of the big companies spend millions of dollars in research and development before they begin to produce new products. We just see the end result and assume that the product is just created and put on the shelf but it's not."

"You're right," she conceded. "It's just that now my juices are flowing I want to launch into making my T-shirts and selling them right away."

"Don't worry, you'll get there. But first you need to get some knowledge about the local and international markets. Find out the size of the industry. You know, how much money is spent on T-shirts worldwide. See who is making what, who will be your competitors, who is specifically making T-shirts with positive messages and so on."

"OK, OK." She held up her hand as if to stop his words. "You're making me feel overwhelmed. But you're right. I know that a lot of companies fail because they rush into business without doing their research and I won't fall into that trap. When I get home I'll go on the Internet and find out what is out there."

"That's good for information on the international markets but what about the local market?"

"I'm not sure. I may have to do some kind of survey of my potential customers and maybe visit stores to see what they carry now."

"Good idea. All that will go into your business plan."

"Business plan?" she groaned again.

"Yes a business plan. You know that start-up companies rarely get bank loans. They are more likely to get family or friends to invest in the business to help get it started but even they will want proof that the business has a chance at succeeding. A business plan is the tool to show them that. It also helps you to get a clear understanding of what your business is about."

"OK. So can you think of anyone, friend," she stressed the last word, "who might be interesting in investing in my business if I prepare a great business plan?"

He laughed and said. "I may know someone who might be interested, if it looks like a good investment."

"What? You're not going to invest in my business unless you see a business plan?" She exclaimed.

"I love you dearly, but I'm a business man as well. I need to make sure I invest my money wisely, with my head and not my heart. So I need to see your business plan. It will also help you to focus on what you're trying to achieve."

"OK. I'll prepare an amazing plan and prove to you that this is a good investment."

"Great! I look forward to reading it."

• • •

Tessa opened Google Chrome and Googled: T-shirt industry. She was excited to see a link saying: Tap into the 40-billion-dollar T-shirt business.

"Wow! I only need a tiny share of that market. "

Feeling encouraged after watching the video that came up, she started searching for the companies that made similar types of T-shirts. There were a number of companies with green messages and other positive messages and several with the kind of designs that she planned to do. She had hoped that they would be very few or none, but Joshua had warned her that if no-one was making a product it was probably because there was not market for it, so it was good that other businesses were making similar T-shirts.

She knew from her personal experience that the local market carried many imported T-shirts, the best of which were from the big brands but there was only one local company she could think of that was doing her kind of T-shirts and even that was not catering specifically to young women. She wondered idly why that was. Could it be that there was no market? She couldn't believe that.

She smiled to herself as she realized that she was doing what her Marketing 101 course called secondary research, which was gathering information based on existing data. That would be useful and necessary to put into the Marketing section of the plan to demonstrate the size of the industry her business would be a part of.

Of course, there was still the need to carry out primary research which meant going directly to her potential customers, especially in the local market, to collect data. To do that she would need to create a questionnaire and conduct a survey to find out if there would be a demand for her products locally. Her sample would include school girls, community college and university students. She could quite easily conduct the interviews at the university but she would either need to get permission to go into the schools and colleges or she would simply wait outside and stop the students as they were leaving and ask them her questions. Maybe she could give them an offer of 5% off their first purchase as an incentive to participate. She could also gather information via e-mail using SurveyMonkey or another survey service and that way she could get her friends to participate and broaden her sample size.

With resolve she sat down to design her questionnaire in such a way that she would get the information that she wanted. She would include questions like:

Was it easy to find good-quality T-shirts?
How often did they buy clothes?
How much money they would spend for a T-shirt?
Which did they prefer? Plain T-shirts or those with messages?
Were they encouraged by positive messages?
What kind of words would encourage them?

She decided to call a couple of her girlfriends and get some input from them. They weren't working either but they were still sending out applications in hope of getting a job. Maybe she could encourage then to think about becoming entrepreneurs as well.

Chapter 4

* * *

The Journey of a Thousand Miles

Tessa was happy with what she had achieved so far. She had, with the help of her friends, finished the questionnaire. She had created a free account on SurveyMonkey and she would send out her survey to friends via e-mail. She also printed some hard copies so that she could do face-to-face surveys.

She had gotten some good information from the Internet about the size of the industry, the fact that it was a growth industry and also, in an unrelated way, she discovered that there was a desire among the youth for positive messages in spite of what the older people believed. The fact that most of her target market practically lived on the Internet gave her the confidence that she could do well online provided that she could find strategies to reach them at an affordable cost, or better yet, free.

Feeling as if she had accomplished a lot, Tessa turned her attention to starting her business plan. She typed in 'Free Business Plans' and a number of sites came up offering business plan templates and a host of others offered free sample plans. She checked out a few of them and chose a couple of the samples for companies in the online clothing retail business which would give her an idea of how hers should look. She knew that Microsoft Word had a business plan template specifically for a start-up business so she decided to use that template to create hers.

She clicked on a link offering advice on how to write a business plan and started to read:

Writing a business plan[3]

Many potential start-up businesses are daunted by the prospect of writing a business plan.

'You got that right,' she thought to herself before continuing.

But it is not a difficult process - and a good business plan focuses the mind as well as helping to secure finance and support.

She smiled slightly as she acknowledged that this agreed with what Joshua had said.

The business plan will clarify your business idea and define your long-term objectives. It provides a blueprint for running the business and a series of benchmarks to check your progress against. It is also vital for convincing your bank - and possibly key customers and suppliers - to support you.

"OK, OK. I'm convinced," she said out loud.

"You saying something to me, Tessa?" asked her mother from the hallway.

"No mum. Just talking to myself."

"Oh. I do that too. Must run in the family."

Tessa turned back to the screen and opened up the Microsoft Business Plan template. Having read through the blurb on the first page she came to the beginning of the plan where she had to write the business name as well as the address and contact information of the business.

"Right, business name…" She stared over the screen of the computer trying to come up with names. It wasn't the first time she was doing this; she had thought about it at the beach but nothing exciting was coming to mind. She thought about creating another survey and sending it to her friends so that they could help her chose a name, but first she had to come up with some to start with.

"Let's see…How about Positive Tees? Or Totally Tees? Terrific Tees?" She sighed. No good ideas were coming.

Just then the familiar Skype ring interrupted her brainstorming. It was Joshua calling. She hit the video call button to connect the call.

"Hi Joshua," she answered in a dejected voice.

"What's the matter?"

"The good news is that I did some market research and created a questionnaire with some help from Lisa and Sharon but now I'm at the beginning of my business plan and I can't even find a name for the business to put on the first page," she moaned.

Joshua smiled to himself but knew that to dismiss her concerns would only upset her so instead he said, "Don't despair. You don't have to do everything in order. Start with the parts that you can write easily and then go back to the more difficult parts later. The name may come to you as you get more into the plan."

"Oh," she said cheering up. "I didn't think of that. I was thinking I should do it in order. Thank you! I feel so much better."

"What would you do without me?" he teased.

"I hope I never have to find out," she said with a smile. "That means I can work on the section describing the business first. Great!"

"What kind of things do you have to write about in that section?"

"It starts with asking what business I will be in and what I will do. Then I have to create a mission statement. It says 'Many companies have a brief mission statement, usually in 30 words or fewer, explaining their reason for being and their guiding principles.'"

"So what is your reason for starting this business? What's your mission?" Joshua prompted her.

"To provide a range of high quality T-shirts with positive messages for young women and teens to encourage them to follow their dreams and be who they were created to be," she rattled off.

"Sounds good! Did you have that written down before?"

"Kind of. When I was trying to come up with a business idea I started jotting down what I was trying to achieve. It probably needs some more work. I find it a bit clumsy."

"Not to me but you have to be happy with it."

"Thanks," she yawned. "I'm feeling really sleepy. It must be all of that sea breeze today."

"Yeah, plus the fact that it's almost twelve."

"I didn't even realize it was so late."

"Time flies when you're having fun," he quoted.

"I don't know about that because I wasn't having that much fun before you called. Anyway, I'll endure preparing this plan because I know that it's putting me closer to actually starting the business. Thank you for encouraging me to think about being an entrepreneur instead of an employee."

"You're very welcome. I don't like seeing you so down. You know my mission in life is to make you happy," he teased.

"That's why I love you."

"Love you too. See you tomorrow."

"Yeah. Tomorrow I'll work on the rest of this section. Bye."

Chapter 5

• • •

More Steps

The day was going to be beautiful. Tessa looked out of her window and could see the blue sky with hardly a cloud in it as the breeze lifted her curtains and blew across her bed through the open window. She lay in bed for a while, enjoying the fact that she did not have to get up and rush to campus. The quiet of the house told her that her parents had left for work. Her mind reached ahead into the day to what she needed to do and she felt a burst of anticipation as she thought about continuing to work on her business plan now that she could tackle the easiest sections. That was enough to make her throw the sheet off and head for the bathroom to get ready for the day.

An hour later, bathed and fed, she took her laptop outside to the patio to continue working on her Business Plan. She began to type:

Company Description

The Company will be in the clothing retail business with the focus on T-shirts and products which will appeal to the same market such as tote bags, wall hangers, door hangers etc.

The Company will create positive messages using Word Art which will be transferred to T-shirts and the other accessories to inspire teenage girls and young women up to about 25 to follow their dreams and fulfil their purpose.

Mission:

To create high quality T-shirts and accessories with positive messages which will inspire young women to pursue their dreams and fulfil their purpose.

Business Philosophy/Values:

Quality
Excellence
Inspiration

'OK, now for the goals and objectives.' Tessa thankfully had come across an excellent Business Plan blog in one of her searches that beautifully described Goals and Objectives.[4]

The writer described a 'goal' as something that you would like to achieve that could be described "subjectively" with no pressure to be specific. He said that it was also perfectly acceptable to use emotional language. However, objectives should use objective language and should follow the SMART rules:

Specific
Measurable
Attainable
Realistic
Timely

Goals:

1. To create beautiful Word Art designs to encourage young girls to pursue their dreams
2. To inspire teens and young women through positive T-shirts and accessories

3. To encourage young girls to pursue their dreams by financing workshops such as "You're Designed to Shine".

She sighed. She was not sure if these were good goals. She would share them with Joshua later and see what he thought.

OK, on to objectives.

1. To create fifty Word Art designs in the first month of operations.
2. To source and import one hundred T-shirts to sell in month two.
3. To create a website and online store to sell T-shirt designs internationally by the end of the first year of operations.

Having come up with a few goals and objectives Tessa decided to move on to writing about the industry. She could always come back to them later. She was able to write a good section on the industry based on the secondary research she had done. She would have to fill in the primary research after she did her survey. She decided to start that the following day.

• • •

Tessa made herself a salad and warmed up some quiches that were in the freezer. There were only a couple more sections of the Company Description that she needed to complete. She would need to decide on the legal form of the business, talk about what would make the business successful and think about business partners or whether she should do it alone.

After lunch she would look at the business' strengths and what competencies or abilities she would bring to it. Then she would need to decide on the legal form of the business that she would choose. With that thought she popped a piece of ham and cheese quiche into her mouth. The crust crumbled in her mouth with a satisfying crispiness and released the flavours of cheese and ham seasoned with onions and pepper.

"Yum," she said around a mouthful and speared some tomato and lettuce covered with dressing on her fork. Life was good!

Idly she picked up the salad dressing bottle and saw that it was made in the US. She wondered how the company had marketed it so that it ended up on her table in the Caribbean. She needed to find out how to do the same with her T-shirts.

Chapter 6

• • •

The Legal Form - Pros and Cons

Joshua hugged Tessa to his chest as they shared a comfortable chair on her patio. They sat in silence enjoying the coolness of the night and listening to the chirping of the crickets from their hiding places in the dark garden.

His warm breath caressed her ear as he broke the silence and asked: "How did it go today?"

"It went well!" she said enthusiastically, sitting up so that she could turn to face him. He was almost sorry that he had asked as he was enjoying holding her against him. Pushing aside his selfish thoughts, he listened attentively as she enthusiastically reported all she had accomplished.

"The only part I haven't written in this section is about the legal form of the business. I vaguely remember studying that for an exam but it was so dry that I just crammed and of course I can't remember a thing I studied."

"Now you see the dangers of cramming," he scolded teasingly.

"I humbly admit that I have learned my lesson so please refresh my mind about the pros and cons of each."

"Yes, ma'am. You can set up a sole proprietorship by registering a business name. That is the cheapest and easiest method and you go to the Registrar of Companies to do it here. In other countries they may have other agencies to do it or you may be able to register online.

"So the pros, as I said, are the low cost and the ease of setting up the business. It means, though, that you and the business are one. The debts of the business are your personal debts but on the other hand what the business owns is yours. When you come to file your personal taxes, you are taxed on the profits of the business plus any other income you earn."

"Got it."

"Most of the small businesses that you see around are probably sole proprietorships. You know like the barbers and hair dressers, the people who do nails, the mechanics and that sort of thing, if they are registered at all. A lot of businesses operate without registering which is not really legal because then they don't contribute to the country by paying taxes and national insurance et cetera."

She nodded.

"The next step up is a partnership which is also cheap to set up but it is advisable to get a partnership agreement prepared, which may cost you. Or I'm sure you can find a sample partnership agreement online and tailor it to suit what you need. The pros and cons are similar but then you have the added factor of working with one or more people which may or may not be a good thing."

"The good thing is if I bring in other people we can split the work and focus on the areas that we're good at," Tessa said. "The bad thing is that we may not share the same business philosophy and that could lead to problems."

"That's why you should sort out those issues before you create a partnership. The agreement should also show how much money is to be put in up front, who is putting in what and how the profit and losses are to be shared."

"Mm. Need to give that some thought. I like the idea of a partnership but it has challenges as well." He nodded.

"Most of the law firms and accounting firms are partnerships. The thing about partnerships is that you are personally liable for the debts and liabilities of the partnership. Each partner is also liable for the debts that the other partners may incur so it's not just about you anymore. Of course, there are now limited liability partnerships which, as the name suggests, limits the liability of some of the partners so that they are only responsible for the debt of the company up to a certain level. Then there is the limited liability corporation."

"Oh yeah, I remember that one. It's where you incorporate a company which is a separate legal entity and can trade in its own name. The debts of the company are also separate from the owner."

"In theory, although sometimes a financial institution may ask for a personal guarantee for a loan. That means if the company can't pay back the loan, the owner will have to pay it back out of their own pocket. The company also files a separate tax return et cetera. This is the most expensive to set up as well because there is a lot more paperwork involved and here you need to get an attorney to sign the documents."

"So which do you think is best?"

"I would tend to go with the cheapest and fastest at this stage and since any money you get will be either investment or loans from family or friends you don't need to worry about separation of assets and liabilities so much. You can always convert it into a company later when you start to make some money."

"That makes sense. Which brings me to my next challenge which I have not dealt with yet: the name of the business! I can't seem to come up with anything catchy. I can't get it out of my mind!"

"Don't worry! Something will drop into your mind when you least expect it. Speaking of which, something just dropped into mine to take your mind off the business plan," he murmured, pulling her close again. The crickets were the only sounds that were heard for a while.

After a few minutes Tessa sat up again. "Where do you get the forms to register the business and all that? Do I have to go to the Registrar of Companies?"

Joshua nearly groaned out loud. He had created a monster. An entrepreneurial monster! It seemed that all Tessa had on her mind was this business. Then he had to smile to himself because he knew that was how he was sometimes too. He would just have to help her to bring balance to her life, as he was learning to do, so that she was not so consumed by her business that her relationships suffered. That happened to far too many entrepreneurs and business people.

Bringing his mind back to her question, he said: "They are on their website. You can complete them online but then you have to print them so that you can sign them and take them into the office since you have to pay there as well."

"Now where were we?" he asked rhetorically, pulling her towards him again.

Tessa smiled and continued where they had left off.

Chapter 7

• • •

In the Trenches

Tessa dropped her bag in the nearest chair and grabbed a glass before heading for the fridge to get a drink. She was parched and tired. Her feet hurt from standing up for long hours interviewing students and her hands were tired from filling in survey questionnaires. This was the third day of her primary research. She had covered the university and the community college the first two days and she had just come back from town and the bus terminal where she felt she could get a better cross section of school girls rather than concentrate on a particular school.

She had interviewed about two hundred students which she felt was a fairly good sample. Next she would have to analyse the information and see what it was saying. She decided to do a combination of an Excel spread sheet to record the "yes" or "no" type questions and the 1-5 type questions as well as the price range questions but the open ended questions she would have to read through and group similar statements before she recorded them in a Word document.

It had been hard work and not everyone was very friendly or willing to spare the time to answer her questions but it had been worth it. She was pleased with herself because she had persevered and not let the rejections stop her from getting the information she needed. Joshua would be proud of her because she was already showing persistence and perseverance, two of the qualities that he had said entrepreneurs should have.

She made herself a sandwich and took it with her drink to the patio to relax a bit before she started to review all the information she had gathered. She groaned to herself as she remembered that she had promised her mother to cook dinner that evening. Her analysis would have to wait until after she cooked. Unfortunately, becoming an entrepreneur did not mean that she didn't still have to help out around the house. She vowed there and then that when she became successful she would hire a helper who could cook to do the chores that she disliked. She didn't see it as being lazy, but as helping to employ people while giving her the time to do the things that she was better at.

Once her business took off she would also be able to hire people to deal with the parts that she did not enjoy which would allow her time to focus on the creative side. Later, as she became famous she would also be called to speak to young girls to encourage them to pursue their dreams and not to let anyone tell them that they could not do anything they put their minds to.

The ringing of the telephone shook her out of her thoughts of the future. It was her mother reminding her to prepare dinner, which brought her back to reality with a jolt.

'I'm getting way ahead of myself anyway,' she acknowledged with a smile as she headed to the kitchen. She had always been a dreamer.

● ● ●

Tessa stood and stretched her back to get out the kinks. She had been sitting at the computer for over two hours putting her information into the spreadsheet she created and reading through the comments.

She was happy to see an emerging trend that the girls she had surveyed were not happy with the T-shirt offerings in the island and most preferred positive messages on their T-shirts instead of a plain shirt. However, she was not overly happy with the price they were prepared to pay for a T-shirt. It was a bit on the low end considering the price that the big brand T-shirts were selling for. It seemed as if people wanted a lower cost alternative, but would she be able to do that?

She would need to do some research into the possible cost of producing the T-shirts. She did not like the quality of the ones that were made locally so to get the very soft cotton tees she would have to import them. That reminded her of what Josh had said about possible duties. How much could duties be anyway? Then she would have to find out how much screen printing would cost. More research! When would she be able to start her business? She had not even finished the Business Plan yet far less come up with the name for her business.

Heading to the kitchen for an after-dinner snack, she mapped out what she would do for the rest of the night. Tomorrow she would call the customs department and find out what duties and other taxes she would have to pay on imported T-shirts. She knew that most of the governments in the region put duties on imported goods to protect local competing industries and also to preserve their foreign exchange. Because T-shirts were also made in the country, she knew that she would have to pay duties but there was no way she wanted to use those T-shirts for her high quality products so she hoped the duties wouldn't be ridiculous. That was probably why the brand name T-shirts were so expensive.

Next, she would have to call some screen printing companies to see how much they would charge to transfer her designs onto screens to put on her T-shirts.

She looked at her survey results again and began to get a little worried when she saw what her sample target market was prepared to pay for a T-shirt. For the first time, doubts began to creep in about the feasibility of her business.

'Now I know first-hand the meaning of the term 'feasibility study',' she thought. 'It's to see whether something is feasible, or makes sense. I hope it makes sense to do this business.'

● ● ●

The Next Day

After running various errands for her mum and for herself most of that day, Tessa was barely able to call the Customs Department before they closed for the day. She was glad to be able to reach an officer who could tell her the tariffs on imported T-shirts. She held the pen in her hand expectantly and began to write down the various charges as the lady called them out. After a while her hand seemed to drag the pen reluctantly as if she didn't want to write any more. Eventually she hung up the phone and held her head in disbelief.

She could not believe the amount of duties and other charges she would have to pay to bring in soft, high quality T-shirts. When everything was added up it would be over 150% of the cost! She had been surprised at how reasonable she had found the prices of blanks online but by the time she got them into the country and paid all the duties, the price would begin to get up there and that was before the cost of screen printing which she discovered was not that cheap and then she had to put on her mark-up. She would have to price her T-shirts around the same price as the major imported brands but based on the results of her survey, her market would not pay that much. Depression began to creep up on her again and tears of frustration ran down her face.

She couldn't find a job and now her business idea did not even look feasible. She thought of all the hours she had put into preparing her Business Plan, which was still not finished anyway, and it only made her cry harder.

Starting a business was not as easy as it looked. She didn't know what to do now.

Chapter 8

• • •

Starting Over

Tessa's mum opened the door to let Joshua in. She had heard Tessa start to cry and was torn between rushing to find out what was wrong and going to answer the door. She was glad to see Josh at the door because she would let him deal with Tessa. She figured it was something to do with this business she was working on anyway because she had been at the computer in her room for ages.

She didn't understand why Tessa was putting herself through all of this agony to start a business. She and Tessa's father were both employees and they did quite well. They may not have their dream jobs but they were making the most of the circumstances and paying the bills. She couldn't understand how Tessa had given up trying to find a job already. After all, it was only six months since she had left university and although jobs were scare she could at least try for a lower-paying job and work her way up.

She shook her head. These university graduates always felt that they would leave university and walk into a high-paying job. She remembered her first job and what she started at compared to what she was earning now. Then again she had to admit that if she was working for herself there would be no limit to what she could earn provided she put in the effort. But she preferred the security of a pay cheque every month. Well, relative security because she had heard rumours about the company downsizing.

Maybe Tessa was doing the right thing after all because there was no such thing as a secure job anymore. Even the government was sending home people.

"Hi, Mrs. Manning. You're home very early."

"Yes, I took a short lunch so I left early. I only just got in myself. Tessa was on the phone and then all of a sudden I heard her bawling in her bedroom. I was just about to go and see what was wrong when you rang the bell."

"Tessa is crying?" Joshua's face creased in concern. He hesitated, not knowing what to do. He wanted to go and comfort her but he did not usually go into her room.

"I know that we don't encourage you to go into her room, but I will make an exception in this case. Leave the door open though," she warned.

He smiled and gave her a quick hug.

"Thanks, mum. You know you can trust me to treat Tessa with respect."

His future mother-in-law smiled. "I hope so," she said.

• • •

Tessa was crying so hard that she didn't hear Joshua come in. Joshua's heart pained him to see her so distraught. He couldn't imagine what had upset her so but he figured it had something to do with the business.

"Sweetheart?" he said, putting his hands on her shoulders.

"Josh? I'm so glad you're here!" she exclaimed in her tear-soaked voice. She stood up and flung herself into his arms, starting to cry afresh.

He led her over to the bed and pulled her onto his lap with his arms around her. She buried her face in his neck and continued to cry. He rubbed a comforting hand up and down her back, soothing her until she stopped.

He pulled a tissue from a box on her bedside table and handed it to her.

"What has you so upset, love? I hate to see you like this."

Tessa gave a good blow and cleaned her nose before launching into her story. "I just called the Customs Department and would you believe that the duties and other levies come up to 150% of the cost of the T-shirt? So while I was getting excited that the blanks were so cheap, by the time I land them here they will already cost a fair amount, with shipping and all that and then the screen printing is another set of money and that is even before I put on my mark up!" She paused for a breath.

Tears welled up in her eyes again as she continued, "But, based on my survey, my market is not willing to pay much more than $40 for a T-shirt. I thought my idea was so good but the reality is that I won't be able to sell my T-shirts at that price and make a profit. Josh, I spent so much time working on this! I stood up for hours doing the surveys until my feet hurt. I've spent hours on the computer doing research and writing my business plan. And for what? So now I can't find a job and this business that I had set my heart on doesn't even look feasible! What am I going to do?"

Josh got another tissue and gently wiped her eyes. "Things may look bad now but it's not the end of the world. You still have some options. The good thing is that you did the market research before you started the business. Can you imagine if you had gone out and brought in 100 T-shirts only to find out when they landed that the duty and taxes were 150% and after you got the designs put on and tried to sell them you realized that your market was not prepared to pay that price?"

She nodded in agreement. "True. Thanks for stopping me from rushing into the business before I was ready."

"That's what I'm here for. I believe that a lot of businesses fail because entrepreneurs don't have a mentor to guide them and advise them about business and share their own failures and successes. Now don't think of this as a failure. Consider this as information you can use to make an informed decision. At least you're not in the league of Thomas Edison."

"How's that?" she asked.

"He is reported to have said 'I have not failed. I've just found 10,000 ways that won't work.'"

"Definitely not," Tessa laughed, feeling better already. She really loved how Joshua always saw the bright side of things and gave her solutions to help her overcome difficulties.

"Now as I said, you have some options. Several, in fact. One, you can continue with your idea to create the T-shirts locally but go after a different market. You may have to target young people in higher income brackets who can afford to pay for a high-priced T-shirt. Or you can stick to the international market and find partners online and have an online store only. Or..." he paused not sure if she would want to hear the last option.

"Or?" she urged.

"Or you can start over with a completely different business idea."

"A different business?" She groaned. "Do you know how much time I spent trying to start this one?" He nodded and let her come to the next step on her own. He could see her mind turning over possibilities.

"What kind of business are you thinking?" she asked.

"I don't have anything specific in mind but I really feel strongly that we should begin to tap into the knowledge industry or the technology market that is growing so fast or at least focus on businesses where we don't have to import things. There are service businesses that can be done online. For example, since you're so good at graphic art, you can create an online inspirational magazine or something which can do what you wanted to do with the T-shirts. You can create an App for that."

"I don't know anything about creating Apps," she protested.

"Aren't you lucky to be engaged to someone in the IT field? I know people who know people," he teased. "You don't actually have to know how to create the App. Your job will be to work with the designer to create the look and then you would be responsible for the content."

She smiled and he could see her mulling it over in her mind. "I am always complaining about not having Caribbean magazines for my age group and even women a little older than me. Hmm…maybe I can create an online magazine for the region if you can set me up with someone to help me create an App for it."

"Absolutely! And it can either be free or you can sell it for a marginal amount of money. The revenue comes from advertising anyway."

"I like that," she said thoughtfully. "And I love crafting words. I like designing brochures and stuff like that. I love fashion and make-up."

"You're into the gym and fitness," he added giving her suggestions of what she could put in her magazine.

"And best of all I don't have to import anything or pay duties, deal with stock and all that. I like it. I like it!" She repeated, throwing her arms around him.

'I like it too,' Joshua thought to himself, hugging her. His Tessa was back.

Chapter 9

• • •

In the Trenches...Again

"Excuse me, would you be willing to do a short survey about magazines?" Tessa asked yet another university student. She had been on the campus for several hours and she was getting hungry and tired.

"Another survey?" replied the girl, smiling. Tessa looked at her blankly.

"You asked me about T-shirts last week."

"Sorry. I didn't remember," she confessed, embarrassed, "but I've interviewed so many people that the faces are a blur."

"That's OK. I can imagine. Are you doing this for a company?"

"No, for myself. I'm doing market research for a business I'm planning to start."

"What happened to the T-shirt idea?"

"My research showed me that it wasn't viable. The T-shirts were going to cost more than my customers were prepared to pay."

"Good thing you found out before you started the business."

"That's what my fiancé told me but it doesn't make starting over any easier as you can imagine. So, can you spare a few minutes?"

"Sure. I'd be happy to do your survey."

"Thanks. OK, do you read magazines?"

"Yes. I love to read magazines but I hardly buy printed ones now. I tend to buy online magazines."

"Perfect!" Tessa exclaimed. "You've answered my next question and that was the answer I wanted to hear,"

The student smiled. "Glad to help."

"How often do you buy? Or do you subscribe for a whole year?"

"I tend to buy one every other month. Or sometimes if I preview one and I like the sound of the articles I would buy it."

"What kind of articles or features are you interested in reading about?"

"Fashion, of course, make-up tips, travel, book and movie reviews..." She paused to think.

"What about health tips and healthy eating suggestions?" Tessa helped her.

"To some extent. I should probably focus on that more. I like inspirational stories about people who have gone through challenging experiences and triumphed." Tessa was feverishly recording all the information.

"And you know what I would like to see? Reviews of YouTube videos or suggestions of helpful or funny ones to watch since there are so many of them."

"Interesting," said Tessa, writing that down. "Are you interested in information about the Caribbean? Places of interest, the history, what Caribbean people are doing et cetera?"

"Definitely! I find that in the Caribbean we don't know enough about what is happening in each other's country. We need to share more information."

"Great! That is very encouraging. One more thing. How much would you be willing to pay for a magazine?"

"I tend to pay around $2.99, so about that."

"Thanks so much. You've been really helpful," Tessa said wrapping up the interview.

"All the best with the magazine. I would definitely buy it if you get it off the ground."

Tessa smiled at her as she left. She was very encouraged by the responses she had gotten today. Not only were students prepared to stop for a few minutes to do the survey but from what she'd heard, most of them were interested in a Caribbean magazine that they could read online. Some had never read an online magazine but liked the idea since it was more "green", not to mention cheaper. Now she could move forward with her new business idea. What was good was that she was able to get responses from a number of different nationalities so she was able to do a Caribbean survey from just visiting one campus. She would also create the survey on SurveyMonkey and get some input from her e-mail list.

She had already done some research to find out the cost of developing an app and, while one company online had quoted from US $10,000 for developing a custom app, she knew that Joshua had a friend who created Apps. Maybe she could get him to do hers for a lot less. Perhaps she could barter and offer him a combination of money and some free advertising for his business in exchange for creating the App.

Yes, that was the way to go. In fact, if she could barter with a photographer as well and promote his work in her magazine in exchange for doing photos at a reduced price that would be great. She smiled to herself as she packed her up questionnaires and her iPad and headed to Joshua's SUV which she'd borrowed for a few hours. Things were definitely looking up.

● ● ●

Joshua pulled into the drive-thru of a popular fast food restaurant and ordered a quick lunch for both of them.

Tessa had not stopped talking since she'd picked him up at his office which was quite near to the campus. He was glad to see that the magazine App idea seemed to be working out better than the T-shirt idea. She also agreed with him when he pointed out that she could also include her inspirational art in the magazine and she would have a wider audience to inspire.

"I'm very excited about this," Tessa exclaimed. "It's amazing how you can be so depressed one week and the next week be on top of the world."

"Welcome to the world of business. In fact, to life in general."

"I'm glad I have you to pull me out of my doldrums," she smiled at him.

"You do the same for me too. It's important to surround yourself with people who will encourage you and be positive when you're feeling down."

"That's so true."

The long line of cars moved forward slowly but eventually they got to the pick-up window, paid and collected their food.

"I have a meeting in an hour so let's eat at my office, OK? If you want to, you can work at my desk or in the meeting room while I go to my meeting and when I come back I can take you home."

"That sounds good. I'll spend some time looking at competing magazines and see what I like about them and what I don't like."

"I'll give you Robert's number as well and you can start to talk to him about what you want him to do for you and how much it will cost. Later on, I can also give you some contacts in the other islands; people you can speak to about advertising in the magazine and also people who can help you with content, particularly the hotels and restaurants who are our clients."

"That would be brilliant! I'll also make a new list of people that I know who can help me with this business idea. I have quite a few friends from the Caribbean who went to campus with me and who I'm still in contact with. They may be able to help me with some content too and of course there's the Internet."

"Before you get too far ahead of yourself, remember to re-write – "

"The business plan," she finished for him.

He smiled and said, "You're learning. The good news is that you can begin with a Business Model Canvas to help you to think about how you want to operate your business. I had actually forgotten about that."

"Oh yes! We learned about that at university. It's a quick and easy way to create your business model."

"Which basically is how you plan to get money from your customers' pockets into yours, in a nutshell." Tessa laughed at the way that Josh summed up what a business model was in a very practical way when it had taken her professor a whole lecture to explain it to them.

"Ok, I'll do that first and then tackle the business plan again."

They reached his office in just a few minutes and, after devouring his lunch quickly, Joshua headed out the door, leaving Tessa sitting at his desk in front of his computer. He gave instructions to his secretary to find Robert McCollin's contact information and pass it on to Tessa and to give her any other help that she needed.

Tessa sat back in Joshua's cushy executive chair with a sigh of contentment. Being in the air-condition was a lot better than being out in the heat on campus conducting interviews and Josh's high-speed computer with the twenty inch monitor was a luxury that she didn't have. With a smile, she clicked on the Google Chrome button.

Chapter 10

• • •

Developing the Idea

"Hello, Robert? This is Tessa Manning, Joshua Patrick's fiancée."

"Hi Tessa, how're you doing?"

"I'm good. Josh gave me your number and said that I should talk to you about developing an App for me."

"No problem. What do you have in mind?"

"I'm thinking of creating an online magazine and I need an App developed for that. However, I know nothing about apps."

"OK. For a magazine you have to create a "shell" app which is really just a means through which your readers will access your issues. In app jargon we call them kiosk apps. Are you planning to use an iOS platform or Android or both?"

"You've lost me already," she told him.

"Android is an operating system which was developed by Google primarily for mobile devices with touch screens. So you can flip, pinch, swipe, tap et cetera. All the things you do on a Smartphone or tablet."

"Like what I do on my iPad."

"Yes but the iPad and other Apple devices use the iOS platform which was developed by Apple."

"Oh. So which do you recommend?"

"It depends on a number of things. Who your market is and what is the main type of device they are likely to use; whether you plan to charge for your app et cetera."

"Well, my market will be the Caribbean initially but I don't want to limit it to just the region and I'm targeting young women and students."

"OK, so more likely than not even if they don't have an iPhone, they will probably have an iPad," he reasoned.

"Yes. In any case I wouldn't read a magazine on an iPhone; I would more likely read it on my iPad."

"True. Then I would suggest you go with the iOS platform but later you may be able to create an Android app as well so that you cover all bases."

"That makes sense."

"Then you can use the App Store to host the kiosk app and to sell your magazine App."

"How much does it cost to put an app on the App store?"

"Only US $99 a year right now."

"That's cheap," she said.

"Yes. You have to register as an App Developer, though, and there is a fair amount of documentation that you have to complete and there is a review process but once that's done it only takes about a week for your App to go live. The biggest cost is really the App creation unless you know how to do it yourself."

"And I don't. Which is where you come in."

"We'll have to sit down together and discuss more fully what you're looking for, but let me just warn you that a custom App will cost you anywhere from US $5000 but as you're Joshua's fiancée I will give you an ease."

"Thanks, Robert. When will you be available to meet?"

"Let me just check my calendar. Next Wednesday morning looks good. Around ten is good for you?"

"Yes. I'll get your address from Joshua. Thanks for all your help. See you next week."

"No problem."

Tessa hung up the phone. She had learned a lot from Robert and she even had a feel for the cost of getting the business started. At least developing the app. She would still need to pay for a lot of other things like the photographers' time, models for fashion shoots and things like that and it would probably be good to get an iMac so that she could work on the layout of the magazine. That would be about another US $2,000.

Tessa Takes the Challenge

My goodness, she could be looking at about US $10,000 – 15,000 to get the magazine up and running! Where would she get that kind of money? Well at least she had $1000 in a credit union that she had saved from doing books for her aunt. She might be able to get two to three thousand from her parents if she was lucky and she had an aunt who had some money and seemed to have nothing to do with it. How much would Josh be able to invest in the business? Assuming that he would invest at all.

She knew that banks and financial institutions hardly loaned money to start-up companies especially those that had no assets that they could put up as security in case they couldn't repay the loan. She certainly had no car, house, equipment, stocks or bonds that she could offer as collateral.

Maybe she could find an angel investor. Where could she find a rich individual who was willing to invest in her start-up? She knew that angel investors usually wanted a share of the company if they invested but she would be willing to give up a share if she had to. After all, a smaller share of a working business was better than all of one that could not get off the ground. Would an angel investor be interested in a magazine app? She wasn't sure. Maybe once the business was up and running they would be more interested.

There was also the possibility of getting funding from her customers by selling ads but she knew that until the magazine was really established that would be difficult. Maybe Joshua could help her there. He had clients in the hotel and restaurant business in some of the Caribbean islands, so maybe he could persuade a few of them to put a small ad in the first magazine or even offer to barter some of his services in exchange for some of the cost of the ad. She hoped so.

When the business began to grow the chances of getting outside finance was better. There were options like venture capital funds or maybe the same angel investors. Once the business was established she could then go to a bank for a loan if she needed to but she hoped that the ads plus revenue from downloads of the app would finance the expansion of the business. She was getting ahead of herself again. There was no point worrying about it now. She would prepare a new business plan to present to anyone who might be interested in investing in the business, including her parents and Joshua. With that she turned on her iPad and started the process of creating her plan again.

'Now, what shall I call the magazine?' She pondered to herself for a moment and then her eyes lit up.

"Caribelle!" she exclaimed aloud.

The door opened and Joshua appeared in the doorway.

"What's Caribelle?" He asked, coming over to kiss her cheek.

"The name of my magazine. Or it will be. Belle means beautiful, lovely et cetera so my magazine will feature everything beautiful in the Caribbean or it could even mean Carib Elle, you know, like the Caribbean version of Elle magazine."

"I like it," he nodded approvingly as he sat in the visitor's chair. "Did you get hold of Robert?"

"Yes. He was really helpful and he even promised to give me a discount because of you," she smiled.

"Glad to hear that my name has some weight," he teased. She rolled her eyes at him.

"We're meeting next week to go through the details but he said that it might be anywhere from US $5000 up."

Joshua nodded, seemingly unconcerned. At least he didn't balk at the amount so maybe that was a good sign.

"That is just for the app creation. I haven't even begun to add in things like a new Mac or paying models or photographers," she said, beginning to get worried again. "That may as well be $500,000 as far as I am concerned since I don't have that kind of money."

"Don't panic. Just create your Business Model Canvas and prepare your Plan and we will see what can happen from there."

His calm approach made her feel better and as she often did, she thanked God for sending this wonderful man into her life. With his help she would start her business.

Chapter 11

• • •

Progress at Last

Robert McCollin operated from a room in his apartment that he had converted into an office. The first thing that caught Tessa's eye was a 27-inch iMac on his workstation. She looked at it longingly, imaging the layouts for her magazine that she could create on it.

Robert was a tall, thin guy whom Joshua had said was the same age as him. They had gone to school together and had both studied IT at university, although different ones. Tessa noticed that he wasn't hard on the eyes either, not that she had eyes for anyone but Josh.

"So, you are the girl who has Joshua's head turned," he said.

Tessa laughed and replied, "I don't know about that."

"Well, turned enough for him to ask you to marry him."

"I suppose so, then."

He gestured to a chair and sat in his office chair saying, "So you want to create a magazine app. Have you got any ideas to show me?"

"Yes, I created a mock-up of what I have in mind. I did it in Illustrator." She opened her folder and took out several pages with her mock-up of the magazine.

"This is good," praised Robert. Tessa smiled. "Let me take some notes on what you would like your readers to be able to do and therefore what I'll need to create. Once I prepare the shell I'll have to show you how to put in the content."

They talked for over an hour, going through other magazine apps and looking at some of the apps that Robert had created. Tessa was very impressed with his talent and the fact that he had a creative side as well as the technical know-how.

"I'm very impressed," she admitted. "I'm almost afraid to ask how much this is going to cost me."

"For you, I'll give the introductory price which is US$5000 as I told you. In addition, I will throw in doing the documentation required by the App Store and I will register your app for you."

"Thank you. Before you do anything, though, I have to make sure I have the funds to pay you so I will have to get back to you on that."

"No problem. You will also need to register the trademark for your magazine name and not just locally but internationally since you'll be selling on the international market."

"I do?"

"Yes. A trademark is a form of protecting intellectual property. It can be a word, name, symbol or device which is used to indicate the source of a product and to distinguish it from other similar products. So you need to trademark the name *Caribelle* so that no-one else can use it."

"Oh. How much does that cost?"

"Not that much. You can get a US trademark for under US$200 and you can do it online. Just Google 'trademark registration'."

"Thanks. You've been a great help. I'll call you in a week or so to let you know if I'll be able to hire you."

"I'm sure that won't be a problem. Your fiancé has a very successful business," he smiled.

"All I have to do is present him with a very compelling business plan."

• • •

Joshua looked up at the sound of a knock on his office door. He had asked his secretary not to disturb him as he was writing a program and he needed to concentrate.

"Sandra, I asked you not to –," he broke off his words as he saw that it was Tessa, with Sandra standing helplessly behind her.

"Hi sweetheart," he greeted her standing up. "What brings you here?"

"Sandra told me you were busy but I could not wait until later to give you this. Ta da!" She said handing him a bound document. Joshua looked at the cover and read the title aloud.

"'Business Plan for Caribelle Magazine'. Impressive cover," he mused.

"Hope inside is as impressive," she murmured uncertainly.

"Have a seat," he invited.

"No, I shouldn't disturb you anymore. Besides, I don't want to see your face when you're reading it."

"OK." He laughed. "How did you get here and where are you off to?"

"I got a lift with Michael Bain. He will drop me back home."

"And who is Michael Bain?" he asked, raising an eyebrow.

"You know, he was on campus with me. He was in my study group."

"Oh." He didn't sound overly pleased.

"He's just a friend," she laughed. "You know I only have eyes for you."

"That doesn't mean I like you out with other men. But I trust you. Hope I can trust him."

"Absolutely. See you later?"

"Definitely. I'll read the plan before I come over."

"Thanks. Love you," she said getting up and leaning over the desk to give him a quick kiss.

"Love you too."

Joshua looked back at his computer as Tessa closed the door behind her. It opened a few seconds later and his secretary poked her head around it.

"Sorry about that, Joshua. I tried to tell Tessa that you didn't want to be disturbed."

"That's OK, Sandra. Tess is an exception. She can disturb me any time."

"I'll remember that."

She closed the door, thinking that Tessa was a very lucky girl to have a man like Joshua.

Josh opened the business plan and turned to the executive summary since his concentration was well and truly broken.

Executive Summary

Caribelle will be an exciting online magazine featuring the beauty of the Caribbean. It will be operated as a registered business initially. The magazine will be the first of its kind in the region and will cater to young Caribbean women, as well as women of the Caribbean Diaspora and others interested in Caribbean lifestyles. The app will be offered in the Apple App Store and sold at US $2.99 per issue, with free previews available for each issue.

Caribelle will be a high quality magazine highlighting the fashions of Caribbean designers; health and beauty tips based on products indigenous to the region; places of interest in the Caribbean; historical information and heritage sites in the Caribbean; inspirational stories of women of the Caribbean and book reviews of regional and international authors. There will also be a section offering reviews of films and YouTube videos by the editor called Editors Picks and a Letter to the Editor section.

Magazines and periodicals generated $39 billion in sales last year. An increasing number of larger traditional magazines have created online versions over the years but to date there are no Caribbean magazines in the App Store. We will, therefore, be the first Caribbean publication in the App Store, targeting the Caribbean-conscious woman who is a user of mobile devices, particularly the Apple iPad, and who shops online.

Initial market research (see Appendix) has indicated that the target market is very interested in this type of magazine and has felt that there has been a lack of information on the Caribbean region and no online magazine which specifically features Caribbean offerings.

We plan to advertise our magazine via Facebook, Twitter and Instagram as well on campus bulletin boards, in gyms and in the in-flight magazines of Caribbean airlines. We will also cross advertise on the websites of designers, photographers and advertisers.

The editor of the magazine will be Tessa Manning and contributors have already been identified in six Caribbean islands so far. The chief photographer will be William Barclay who will be responsible for coordinating photographers in other islands. Tessa Manning has an honours degree in Business Administration and has experience as a Graphic Artist. She has been an avid reader of magazines for years and has a passion for all things Caribbean. She has over 2000 Facebook friends and about 500 followers on Twitter from all over the Caribbean. The business will be operated from her home initially.

The company is seeking US $15,500 to be spent as follows:

Development of App - $5000
Purchase of iMac - $2000
Salaries and professional fees (three months) - $8000
Registration fees and trademark - $300

Joshua smiled. He flipped through the rest of the document and was impressed by the effort that Tessa had put into it, especially the market research and the mock-ups of the magazine. He would invest in the business and help her to get it off the ground. He was sure that by the end of three months, she would have generated enough of a following to sell some decent ads in the magazine and from there on, the revenue from the ads would cover the administration costs and the app sales would just be gravy. He didn't see *Caribelle* as just a magazine but as a strategy to unite the Caribbean in a way that had not been successfully done before. He was sure that Tessa could get on TV and on radio stations around the region to promote the magazine. He knew people who knew people so he could make a few calls. His girl was about to become an entrepreneur.

Chapter 12

• • •

A contract? You're joking!

Tessa eagerly opened the door to Joshua. She hoped he had read her business plan. Her eyes lighted on the document in his hands.

"Hi, hon," she kissed his cheek and stepped back to let him in.

"Hi, love. I won't keep you in suspense. I read it and I'm very impressed with the level of work you did and the presentation of the plan. In fact, I was so impressed that I've decided to invest in your business..."

"Yaay!" She interrupted, exclaiming childishly, making Joshua smile.

"... so I've prepared a contract for you to sign."

"A contract?" She asked puzzled.

"Let's go somewhere that we can discuss it."

"OK. We can sit on the patio."

They settled down on a sofa and Joshua took out a document and said, "This is the contract that I prepared."

"You want me to sign a contract with you?" She asked in disbelief. "You don't trust me?"

"It's not that I don't trust you but I want you to get into the habit of using contracts in your business, no matter who you're doing business with. It may save you a lot of grief in the future. A contract is a legally binding agreement between two parties. It outlines the terms of the agreement so that there are no misunderstandings."

"Oh, OK."

"I'm going to pay for Robert's services. That will be my investment."

"You're giving me US $5000?" She asked in amazement.

"Not exactly giving. Investing. In exchange I want a share of the business and I will want my investment returned in five years. I've put all that in the contract so I want you to take time and read it through and if you agree with it we can both sign it."

"I will. My parents have agreed to give me a few thousand dollars as a gift so I'll be able to buy my iMac."

"Hold on. One of the things I've put in the contract is my involvement in the business. I won't tell you how to run your business but I would like to have some input and help you make the best decisions. Agreed?"

"Agreed."

"So is buying the Mac up front the best decision? Bear in mind that you will have to pay models and a photographer for the fashion section and people for their contributions and you may not have much revenue from ads yet."

"True," she agreed a bit reluctantly as she had been looking forward to the new computer.

"When the money begins to flow, in a few months or so, then you can buy the iMac. That is a mistake that a lot of start-up businesses make. They want everything up front and end up spending money they can't really afford and then they find themselves struggling for cash later."

"You're right. I guess I don't need the Mac right away. And did I say "Thank you" for your investment?"

"Actually you didn't. You said 'Yaay!'"

She laughed and then said very seriously, "Thank you for investing in my business and for believing in me."

"You're very welcome, sweetheart. I know that you will do well."

● ● ●

The Next Day

Tessa couldn't wait to call Robert to tell him that he could get started creating the app and barely restrained herself until nine to call him. Robert said that he was glad Joshua had decided to pay for the app because he was looking forward to creating a high-class magazine app and he was sure it would take off.

"I have a couple of projects to clear off my desk and then I'll be able to get started on yours in a couple of days."

"No problem," Tessa told him. "That will give me time to start planning the first issue. I want to be able to hit the market in a couple of months so I need to sit down and work out how I will do that."

"Sounds like a plan," he agreed.

Tessa hung up the phone and turned back to her computer. Although she had prepared the business plan, she was going to spend some time creating a short term plan of things she needed to do in the next couple of weeks to get the magazine ready for the market. She would create action plans with deadlines to force herself to get things done within a particular timeframe so that she would be on target with her start date. She knew that if she didn't set deadlines for herself very often things would not get done.

She decided to divide her plan into four parts:

Administration, which would cover the things pertaining to the business that she needed to put in place, like the registration of both the business name and the trademark, preparing contracts for the contributors etc.

Content Development, which would mean connecting with her contributors, who were really fellow students locally and in other islands, to discuss and agree on their assignments and their deadline dates.

Marketing and Advertising, which would involve working to promote the magazine, creating a poster which would incorporate the initial cover and meeting people about advertising at their locations and on their websites etc.

Revenue generation, which would focus on trying to get ads for the first edition. She would start with people she knew since it was usually easier to deal with people that you already had a relationship with and they were more likely to support you.

With that in mind she started creating action plans that she needed to carry out in each section and set herself deadlines. Like most small businesses, she would have to deal with all the areas herself until the business got big enough to hire staff. Then she would be able to assign people to look after the marketing for the business, the finances, and to handle the administration, which she hated. She would deal with the production herself, which, in the case of the magazine, was content development.

Speaking of which, she reminded herself, the first order of business was to go down to the Registrar of Companies and register her business so that she could create a logo and a letterhead to use when she prepared her contracts and other correspondence. She would do that in a couple of hours.

The creation of the magazine was calling to her so, once she finished her plan, she started conceptualizing what the first issue would look like and the kind of articles and features it would contain. She could hardly wait to see the end product. A feeling of satisfaction and achievement came over her and she smiled to herself as she realized that she was truly about to launch a business and be on her way to becoming an entrepreneur. Why didn't she think of it before? She may not be manufacturing a product and shipping it to other countries but at least she was using her gifts and abilities to create something which would be available in the Caribbean and worldwide for anyone who wanted to buy it. Not only would it generate revenue for her and foreign exchange for the country but she hoped that by highlighting the Caribbean, the magazine would cause more visitors to want to come to the region to experience for themselves what they would read about in *Caribelle*.

Chapter 13

• • •

Another Entrepreneurial Venture

Two Weeks Later

The time flew by like a whirlwind. Tessa registered her business, set up a bank account, set up the accounts for her business on QuickBooks and contacted her contributors to confirm their assignments, agreed on their fees and gave them deadlines. She was waiting for Robert to get back to her with the initial development of the app. She didn't want to start calling potential advertisers until she had the app designed so that they could see what the magazine would look like so she felt a bit at a loose end.

She was thrilled to receive the very first contribution for her magazine from one of her contributors, her friend Maggie from Dominica. Maggie had e-mailed it to her only last night, way before her deadline, but Maggie had always been like that from campus days. While Tessa was often working on assignments until the day they were due, Maggie would have hers finished and neatly bound, at least two days before the due date. That was one of the reasons she had chosen her as a contributor; she knew that getting her information would not be an issue. She couldn't say the same for all of her contributors, though, and she hoped they would not stress her out by waiting until the last minute to send in their information.

The feature that Maggie sent was about a young entrepreneur who had started making soaps from natural products in order to earn some extra money since she did not work for very much. The soaps started to sell so well and the demand was so great that she eventually quit her job and began to operate her soap business full time. Tessa felt inspired and encouraged even as she read the article:

"In the same was that we say 'Pass a Kleenex' when we want a tissue or we say 'Q-tips' to mean earbuds, the name *Savon Naturel* has become synonymous with natural soaps in Dominica. The business was started by Candace Balmain just about two years ago and has taken off beyond her wildest dreams.

"It wasn't that easy in the beginning," admits Candace, "because I was still working and having to make the soap at night and on the weekends. But I started taking a few bars to work and the girls all went crazy over it and told me how good it was and that it was a good price as well. Then they started buying some to give as gifts and the people that they gave it to wanted more. So my customers found out about my soap by word of mouth so I didn't have to advertise it. At first I was making just one kind and that was an experiment to tell the truth, but now I'm doing five different varieties and testing out new products, textures and scents all the time. I've found that people are getting more and more into natural products which is why I think mine have done so well. And because the price is quite reasonable, they are willing to buy even though they cost a little more than normal bath soap."

This creative young lady, who is only twenty-three, told us that she never thought that she could run a business and, although she was always good at making things and she always had an interest in natural products, it was hardship, more than anything else, that had forced her into business. But now she wonders why she had not thought of it before.

She uses local products like virgin coconut oil, ground up noni seeds, shredded coconut, aloe and various other ingredients in her soaps. These are supplied by local small farmers and she has started importing shea butter which she uses in her moisturizing soaps.

"Getting quality raw material when I need it has been a challenge, especially when I started to expand, but I have recently entered into arrangements with some larger suppliers who are more reliable. I want to help out the small suppliers but they need to be more consistent and I can't run a business properly if I can't depend on my suppliers. I enjoy working with other creative young people as well. A friend of mine introduced me to a girl who created the packaging for the soaps and I'm very happy with it! The Accountant at the place I used to work helped me to work out the cost of the soaps so that I would know how to price them. She also introduced me to a lady who runs a spa and she has not only bought a lot of my products but she has become my mentor and has helped me to set up my business properly and to deal with the many issues that I run into daily.

"One of the things she taught me was the importance of promoting my products and not just relying on people coming to me. So I have done a few promotions at fairs and markets where I set up a table and give away small samples and sell products. I was also very grateful when our local newspaper was doing a feature a few months ago on local manufacturers and included me as that also helped my sales. I've been able to take on two members of staff; one to help with production and one to help distribute the products as well as deal with suppliers and clearing material from the port."

One of the challenges that Candace encountered as the business began to expand was the need for a proper manufacturing facility. She had started out at home but as demand for her products grew, she could no longer operate from there and also needed new equipment to increase her production. Fortunately, she was able to get a grant from a local development agency which enabled her to rent a small space in a warehouse and buy the equipment she needed to upscale her business.

Her big break came when one of the hotels heard about her products and, after taking some samples, contracted her to supply smaller versions of her soap to be used as part of the in-room amenities. The hotel also purchased a few of the regular-size bars to carry in their gift shop in case visitors asked where they could get the soap. As a result, one of the guests who was from Germany expressed interest in importing some of the soaps to sell in her own spa in Germany.

"I am very excited at the prospect of exporting my soaps to Germany. When I started my business I never dreamed it would have grown so quickly or that people in other countries would even be interested in my products. I've started taking some evening courses as well so that I will be more knowledgeable about keeping my books properly and marketing the company, especially using the Internet. Running a business can be challenging but I love it and having a mentor has helped me a lot. I encourage all young people not to only think about looking for a job but to consider starting their own business. There is nothing like it!"

Tessa put down the paper with tears in her eyes. This was exactly the kind of article she had hoped for. It was definitely Caribbean, the products were made with local produce and the business was on the brink of exporting and would be earning foreign exchange. Perfect! If all the other content was as good, *Caribelle* would definitely be a success. She was still smiling when the phone rang.

"Hello," she sang into the phone.

"Hi, Tessa. You sound very happy." It was Joshua.

"I am! I just read the first contribution for the magazine and it's perfect. Everything I had hoped it would be."

"That's great! Looking forward to reading it. I realised that we've both been so busy I forgot to tell you that my company is having a retreat next week. The whole staff is going to stay at a hotel on the East Coast for a couple of days to do some team building and we have a consultant coming to facilitate our strategic planning process and help us to take the company forward."

"Oh! I won't see you for two whole days?" she whined teasingly.

"I was actually thinking that you should come so that you can see how companies operate as they begin to grow and take on employees. It's one thing working on your own but when you begin to take on staff there are a whole other set of issues to deal with."

"That sounds great! I really can't afford to pay for a hotel right now, though."

"I invited you so I wouldn't expect you to pay."

"Ok, great! In that case I would love to come. Who knows? In a few years I might have to do this."

"True. So what is the article about?"

"It's a feature on a young entrepreneur in Dominica who started making natural soaps from her house a couple of years ago and now her business has taken off and she may have the opportunity to export to Germany!"

"That sounds good. That's exactly what we need in the Caribbean and maybe when women from the region read about her, she'll get some calls for her products in the other islands."

"That's exactly what I'm hoping for with this magazine. That it won't just be for entertainment but it will educate us about what is available in the Caribbean and, therefore, cause us to start buying from each other more. So we're going to make it a point to include contact information and websites et cetera of all the people and businesses that we feature."

"I like that! CSME in action. This magazine is going to be huge!" He predicted.

"I hope you're prophetic..." she began laughing.

"Yeah, and not pathetic," he finished, knowing what she was going to say.

"True. I'm going to tell my mum about the retreat. I can just hear her now: 'Just as long as you're not sharing Joshua's room'."

He laughed. "Not that it's not a tempting thought, but I respect your decision to wait until we get married, which by the way, needs to be soon."

"I agree. Maybe we can talk about that if we have some time alone at the retreat."

"In that case, I'll make sure that we do."

Chapter 14

• • •

Growing the Business

Joshua, his partner and the team had just gone through some physical exercises to build trust and bonding in the team. It had been a fun morning and having had a light snack they were ready to start working on the Five Year Strategic Plan.

"Although you're planning for the next five years, you have to be flexible and work in the context of the uncertainty we're operating in. That means rather than planning in a fixed way, like saying you want to achieve a particular goal and then trying to figure out what you need and who you need to achieve it, you need to look at what you have now and who you know and work those things into where you want the company to be in the next five years."

Joshua and Tessa looked at each other and smiled.

"That sounds familiar, oh wise one," Tessa whispered to him.

Their attention was drawn back to Andrea, the consultant facilitating the planning session.

"Before we start, I'd like to get a sense of how the company is organized and how effectively that is working right now. Joshua, perhaps as the CEO you can draw a rough organizational chart of the company."

"No problem," he said, getting up and heading towards the flip chart. He quickly drew an organization chart showing the relationships of the people in the company and who reported to whom. As Chief Executive Officer or

CEO he was at the top of the chart. In other companies this position was also known as the President or the Managing Director.

He explained his role to Andrea as leading the company generally and making strategic level decisions and ensuring that they were carried out. He was also responsible for managing the resources of the company and building relationships with key decision makers in their target market.

"That's why I play so much golf," he excused himself.

Tessa smiled to herself as she thought about that. She would have to learn golf if she wanted to network at that level too.

"I also write programs to enhance the packages that we sell and maintain because that is something that I love."

His partner, Shawn, who owned 40% of the company, was the VP of Finance, Marketing and Operations. In big corporations these duties would have been split into three separate positions. He was more involved in the day-to-day operations of the company such as dealing with clients and overseeing some of the marketing and the administration of the company as well as the finances. As the VP of the company, Shawn reported to Joshua.

Under him there was an Office Manager who dealt with the administration of the business as well as human resource issues and the Accountant who looked after the preparation of the financial information together with an assistant who did the day-to-day data entry. The four consultants who served the clients, and were at the core of the company's business, reported straight to Shawn and Joshua's secretary reported directly to him. They were also responsible for building relationships with people at their level in the industry, like Food and Beverage Managers, Front Office Managers etc. so that they could market their products and services to them. So there were eleven people in the company including the lady who cleaned.

"Ok, thanks Joshua. That is good," Andrea said. "Let's talk about how things work in the company."

"They actually work very well," Joshua said.

"I should get the staff's opinion on that," Andrea teased and everyone laughed.

"Actually it's true," confirmed Shawn. "Although we have a formal reporting structure and we do follow it, we tend to take a very team-based, cross-functional approach. That means although I have separate meetings with the consultants, we also have meetings with all the other staff so that we know what is happening in other parts of the company and how what we do impacts on the others."

"Yes, so if we're running low on money, I remind them that when they're late submitting their time sheets, I can't bill clients and that means money is slow in coming in and, therefore, they won't be able to get paid," chipped in the Accountant.

"We're also able to understand Joshua's role better when we get new clients so we don't resent the amount of time he spends on the golf course, which he says is for work purposes," added Shawn teasingly.

"I can attest that it's work," supported Joshua's secretary who usually made the arrangements.

"And what kind of leadership style does Josh have?" asked Andrea.

"Should I leave the room?" Josh joked. Everyone laughed.

"No, you need to hear this. Let me explain the different styles and you can tell me which Josh uses and if it's working," said Andrea. "There are so many different styles that people use but I like Daniel Goleman's from 'Leadership That Gets Results'. He describes six different styles: Coercive or Commanding which says "Do what I tell you"; Authoritative which says "Come with me"; Affiliative which says "People come first"; Democratic which says "What do you think?"; Pacesetting which says "Do as I do now" and Coaching which says "Try this"."

"That's a lot to digest," said Joshua's secretary, "but I think Joshua's style is Coaching. He's always encouraging me to develop myself and try new ways of doing things."

"I think he's authoritative or visionary," said Shawn. The consultants nodded as well. "He's always seeing the future and tries to get us to see it and to buy in. But then again maybe he's democratic because he often asks me what I think."

"He can be commanding sometimes," said the Accountant, "especially when it comes to dealing with the finances and collecting money from clients."

"Anybody disagrees or sees any other styles?" Andrea asked. The others shook their heads.

"Well that is actually very good," she assured them, "because good leaders exhibit different styles depending on the circumstances, but the ones which generally have a positive impact are authoritative, democratic and coaching. In fact, the authoritative leadership style is the most strongly positive. Many leaders don't have time for coaching which is probably why Josh's secretary is the one who more sees that side of him since she is in contact with him the most, I would imagine. Now, would you say Josh is a good leader?" She continued.

"This is definitely where I need to leave the room," Josh said, pretending to rise. "I don't know if my ego can take this." Everyone laughed.

"Many things determine if someone is a good leader or not. For example, if they have vision, if they're flexible, if they can communicate well and so on," offered Andrea.

"I think things like being humble enough to listen to staff is also a good quality in a leader," said one of the consultants.

"Also the ability to make tough decisions. That requires courage," said the Office Manager.

"So, is Joshua a good leader based on the qualities you just told me?" There were murmurs of agreement all around.

"Whew!" Josh exclaimed, pretending to wipe his brow. "I was getting a little worried there." Everyone laughed. Tessa looked at Joshua and saw the respect that his team had for him and the rapport that they had and she was proud of what he had achieved in his company.

"OK, it sounds as if you're doing a lot of things right," praised Andrea. "Now let's talk about where you want the business to go. This is where your visionary leadership style can take over. Before we do that, we should probably take a coffee break because we all need to be alert for this. Shall we say twenty minutes?"

Chapter 15

• • •

What's the Purpose of this Business?

Twenty Minutes Later

"**O**K, welcome back," greeted Andrea. "I'll turn it over to Joshua now to talk a little about the mission and vision of the company and then we'll work on creating the new vision and how we will achieve that. Remember that the mission stays the same but the vision changes with time and circumstances."

"Thanks Andrea. Before we start to work on where we want to take the company, let me share a bit more about what we do so that you will have a better understanding of our business.

"As you know, we are the agents for software which has been specifically designed for hotels and restaurants. The software captures front-end information such as reservation information in a hotel or meals and drinks in a restaurant and it feeds that information into the back-end, which includes the accounting and inventory functions. But it can also be used for marketing purposes. There is also an HR component to the software. In fact, it covers all aspects of the business.

"So, we sell Management Information Systems software which helps management to make effective decisions based on timely and reliable information. In some cases the software provides exactly what they need and sometimes I have to write a program to integrate the package with another report they may require. Of course, Management Information Systems are only as good as the data that is input and the procedures that they use to capture the data so it's up to the client to make sure that they properly deal with that aspect of the system. They also have to have the right hardware to run the programs and people in place to enter the information. And that is it in a nutshell."

"Thank you, Joshua. That has been useful," Andrea said. "OK, let's talk about the mission and vision of the company. Just to make sure that we're all on the same page, the mission tells the purpose or reason for the existence of a business. The vision gives a picture of where it wants to be or to look like at a particular time in the future. For example, Ford's vision is 'To become the world's leading consumer company for automotive products and services'. Nike's is 'To be the number one athletic company in the world'. Joshua, perhaps you can refresh everyone's memory about the mission and vision for the company."

He nodded.

"Well, you all know, or should know, that the mission of the company is 'To provide IT solutions that enhance our clients' businesses while providing a work environment that brings out the passion in our people'. Our vision for the last five years has been to dominate the local market and we've done that. My vision for the next five years is to do the same regionally. We've already got a presence in some of the smaller islands because we really have no competition in their markets but I want to target the bigger countries now, like Trinidad and Jamaica, and even some of the smaller countries, like St. Maarten and Aruba, which have a high level of tourism. I would like to partner with companies in those countries to do that."

"Great! What we need to do now is to see how we can go about achieving that vision. Now, as I alluded to earlier, in the past when there was less uncertainty companies would come up with goals and then try to see what they needed to do to achieve them in terms of people, equipment, money et cetera. Because of the times that we're in now, entrepreneurs tend not to operate that way. Instead, they look at what they have already in terms of skills, people, products and services and who they know, whether it be existing clients, business colleagues et cetera and then they try to figure out how they can use those things to get where they want to go."

Tessa realized that it sounded a lot like what Josh had told her to do in her stocktaking process. It was beginning to make a lot of sense.

"Not that setting goals is not important," continued Andrea, "because goals do help you to plan but I recently read an article that made me think differently about setting goals. It was called 'Forget Setting Goals. Focus on This Instead'[8] and the writer was saying that rather than setting goals and trying to achieve them, you can achieve your goals by creating a system and when you consistently work your system, you will achieve your goals. So, in the case of your company, you want to expand into the region, so rather than creating a goal that says you want to be in three new countries within a year, you need to create a system for making new contacts in the region and finding ways to market your business so that you will achieve your goal of getting business in three new countries. Do you get what I mean?"

"I'm not sure I understand that practically," Tessa admitted. "Can you give me a non-business example to see if I can get my head around it?"

"Sure," Andrea said. "Here's a practical example. Suppose you set yourself a goal to lose twenty pounds in three months. That sort of goal can put you under pressure and cause stress and, in any case, it makes you focus only on the 20 pounds. However, if you put a system in place in which you begin to eat healthier and you go to the gym three times a week, you will eventually lose the twenty pounds without the stress of it hanging over your head."

"OK. I get it. Creating a system and following it will require a lot of discipline, though."

"Absolutely!" Andrea agreed. "OK, let's get back to your business, Joshua. What do you already have and who do you know?"

The rest of the time until lunch was spent doing stocktaking for the company, as Joshua had called it, and it was quite surprising to find that between them there were a lot of resources in the company and contacts that they did not even know each person had.

Tessa was very impressed with the facilitator and the way she drew information from the staff over the weekend and how they worked together to put plans in place to achieve what they wanted to do. She could see from the enthusiasm that everyone showed that Joshua's mission 'to bring out the passion in his people' was alive and well and that everyone was on-board with the vision that he had and was committed to finding ways to achieve it. She looked forward to the day when her company would be big enough to hire people and hoped that she would be able to instill in them the same passion for her vision that Joshua was able to do with his staff.

Chapter 16

• • •

Not All Roses

Six Weeks Later

Tessa clicked on the red phone on her Skype screen and held her head in her hands. She would have loved to be on a real phone to have the brief satisfaction of slamming it down, not that it would help. She could not believe how much trouble she was having getting all the information from her contributors; friends who said that they would have no problem meeting their deadlines!

She had received the photographs from three of the four photographers who had done fashion shoots in their islands but one still had not sent his. Should she pull his shots and just go with the other three? She had really wanted to include that designer, though, since she had heard so much about her line of clothing.

She was also waiting on an article about the benefits of virgin coconut oil which would go well with the feature on Candace Balmain and she had found recipes with virgin coconut oil to include on that page. She should just go on the Internet and pull together the information herself. Unfortunately, she had paid her friend up front since she was having cash flow problems.

Relying on other people was a pain, she was finding out. Everyone did not operate with the same level of excellence and definitely not the same level of urgency. No way would she pay people up front for work again. She would at least pay 50% if she had to, and that was only if she had to. It didn't matter if they were friends or not. In fact, she needed to start looking for other contributors who were not friends because she was finding out that doing business with friends was not always the best thing. It could definitely put a strain on the friendship when she had to deal with issues like late submission and payment on delivery of the articles.

She had told the advertisers she had convinced to buy space in the first issue that she would be ready to launch at the beginning of July so that they would get the summer reading crowd and she could not even get all the articles that she needed! That was only one side of the issue with the advertisers; the other was getting money out of their hands and into her back account.

She had been happy to be able to attract some of Joshua's clients, particularly one of the world-renowned luxury hotels. She knew it was really because of their relationship with Joshua that she had gotten their business but she was still waiting for payment. Granted, Joshua had warned her about that particular client and how long they took to pay but she had been so intent on getting them on board to boost the image of the magazine that she hadn't really thought through what it would mean for the business to have to wait that long for payment. Obviously she was not going to be able to pay herself that month, not when she had to pay her contributors and photographers.

Why did she think that this would be a breeze? Should she have stuck it out longer and tried to find a job? She had to admit that those thoughts often crept up on her, especially when her parents made little comments like 'Why are you putting yourself under all this pressure?' and 'How much money do you think you will make?' and 'Do people actually buy magazines that they can't hold and turn the pages?'. She knew that they didn't really intend to be insensitive but they just did not understand her dream and her desire to make her own way in business rather than relying on a salary like they were doing.

She was so glad that she had Joshua to encourage her. He had started taking her with him to networking forums so that she could begin to meet other entrepreneurs and talk to them about business and begin to get known in the market so that she could create her own network. That way she could build up her own list of advertising clients and feature some of their products and services in her magazine.

She quickly found Joshua's Skype address and called him. She needed a dose of his optimism and encouragement. The familiar Skype ring was soon interrupted by Joshua's voice and face on the screen. She drank in his good-looking face eagerly.

"Hi, love," he said. "What's up?"

"Oh Joshua, this is so hard! Sorry to bother you at work but I can't talk to my parents about it because they don't understand why I'm doing this and most of my friends are still looking for a job."

"Having a hard day?"

"That is the understatement of the year!" exclaimed Tessa. "I can't seem to get the last two contributions I need to finish this magazine to get it out on time. I'm supposed to go live in two days and every time I call Alexis and Mark they keep putting me off and telling me they'll get their information to me soon! They seem to have no sense of urgency."

"Can you leave them out of this edition?"

"I can probably leave out Mark's photos, although I really don't want to, but Alexis' article is crucial because it ties in with the one on the soaps in Dominica and I've created three recipes to go with the product that she's reporting on." She groaned in despair.

"Look, you can't do anything more right now, so I suggest you get out for a bit and get a change of scenery. Relax and come back to it later. Then send them an e-mail, highlighting what they agreed to in their contract and give them a last warning."

"OK. I just didn't want to go there but I guess I'll have to. I plan to find other contributors because this friendship thing is not working out."

"I know that I've been helping you through stuff but I think you need a mentor, someone who has experience in your industry. There's a friend of my mum's who used to be an editor of a magazine in New York and she's just come back home after her retirement. I don't know why I didn't think of it before. I'll introduce you to her and see if she would be willing to be your mentor. She would be perfect for you."

"Oh, that sounds great Joshua. I hope that she agrees. Then I can stop whining to you and call her instead," she smiled, feeling better. It was amazing how talking to Joshua lifted her spirits but she couldn't rely only on him. A mentor in her industry would be perfect.

"Thanks, Joshua. You have been such a help to me in starting this business. You must be tired of hearing me say 'I don't know what I would do without you'."

"I'll never get tired of hearing you say that," he assured her. "I'll give my mum a call this evening and get the information for her friend. Or better yet, you can call her. She said that she hasn't seen you recently now that you've become a hotshot entrepreneur."

Tessa laughed. She really loved Joshua's mum. "I don't know about hotshot entrepreneur, but she's right. I haven't seen her for ages. I'll call her right now."

"OK, love. See you later."

"Bye." Tessa disconnected the video call and smiled. Joshua always put things into perspective. Everyone should have a Joshua to help them with their business.

• • •

Epilogue

The Following Week

"**H**i Tessa," Josh greeted her as she opened the door.

"Hi Josh!" She reached up to kiss him on the cheek.

"Wow! You look beautiful," he praised.

"You did say to dress up because you were taking me somewhere special for dinner when you called today. What's the occasion?"

"This," he held up a newspaper in his hand. "I'm sure you haven't seen the business section of this newspaper yet or you would have called me screaming," he laughed.

"Why? What's in it?"

"Have a look," he offered, giving her the paper.

Tessa's eyes quickly scanned the page that Josh had opened and her heart caught in her chest as she saw the heading:

First Caribbean Magazine App launched on Apple App Store

Readers are in for a treat when they buy the debut edition of Caribelle, the first Caribbean Magazine App on Apple's App Store. The magazine is the brain child of Tessa Manning, a young, bright entrepreneur who decided to start her own business when she could not find a job after graduating from university with a BSc in Business Management.

The magazine is a delight of fashion, travel, health, cuisine and special features about Caribbean entrepreneurs, such as Candace Balmain, this month's featured entrepreneur, who is making high quality natural soaps in Dominica and is about to start exporting to Germany.

A source close to the founder says that her vision for the magazine is to educate Caribbean people about each other and to promote trade between the islands by highlighting the high quality of goods and services that are produced in the region.

The app for this attractive, high-quality magazine was designed right here in the island under the creative direction of Miss Manning, which just goes to show the kind of talent that we have locally. We wish the team at Caribelle all the success and we expect to hear great things about the magazine in the months and years to come.

"Wow!" Tessa said in awe. "I can't believe I've actually done it! I started my own business and it's up and running and getting good reviews. I wonder who 'the source close to the founder' is." She smiled, turning to Josh.

"Just call me The Source," he teased.

"Thank you so much for all your help, Josh. Not to mention your investment. If you hadn't put the idea to start a business in my mind in the first place I may still have been looking for a job. I wish that young people all over the world had someone to encourage them and to let them know that entrepreneurship is not just for a select few. It's for anyone who's can come up with an idea or act on an opportunity and is prepared to work hard at their business. You don't have to be born an entrepreneur. With persistence, perseverance and passion plus encouragement, like you gave me, we can all be entrepreneurs."

• • •

PART II – THE ABC's

Chapter 1

• • •

Entrepreneur or Employee?

Sometimes people leave university and cannot find a job or they are made redundant from their job and are forced to make the decision whether to continue to look for a job and become an employee or become an entrepreneur.

What is an entrepreneur or entrepreneurship? There are many definitions, some are:

1. A person who organizes and operates a business or businesses, taking on greater than normal financial risks in order to do so. (Google)
2. An entrepreneur is a person who organizes and manages a business undertaking, assuming the risk for the sake of profit.[1]
3. Entrepreneurship is a process of identifying and starting a business venture, sourcing and organizing the required resources and taking both the risks and rewards associated with the venture.[2]
4. Entrepreneurship is the pursuit of opportunity beyond resources controlled "Pursuit" implies a singular, relentless focus.
"Opportunity" may entail 1) pioneering a truly innovative product; 2) devising a new business model; 3) creating a better or cheaper version of an existing product; or 4) targeting an existing product to new sets of customers.

"Beyond resources controlled" implies resource constraints (Professor Howard Stevenson, Harvard Business School)

There are different types of descriptions given to entrepreneurs. Here is a sample:

1. The Serial Entrepreneur is a person who continuously comes up with new ideas that they turn into business opportunities.
2. The Social Entrepreneur drives social innovation and transformation in various fields including education, health, environment and enterprise development. This type of entrepreneur pursues poverty alleviation goals with entrepreneurial zeal, business methods and courage to innovate and overcome traditional practices. (Schwab Foundation for Social Entrepreneurship)
3. Lifestyle Entrepreneurs create a business with the purpose of altering their personal lifestyle (such as having flexible hours, spending time with family, fulfilling work, creative pursuits etc.) and not necessarily for profits. Their business is usually based on a passion that they have for a particular product or service so they combine their personal interests into a business they love doing.
4. The Idealist Entrepreneur is an innovator and enjoys working on something new or creative, or something personally meaningful.
5. The Optimizer Entrepreneur is content with the personal satisfaction of owning his/her own business.
6. The Hard Worker Entrepreneur enjoys working long hours to build a larger, more profitable business. He/she likes the challenge it presents and reaps the rewards if the business turns out to be a multi-million dollar enterprise.
7. The Wealth Creation Entrepreneur creates a business with the ultimate goal of reaching the largest available market whilst making the highest profit.

Below are examples of two of these types of entrepreneurs.

The Social Entrepreneur

Francine Charles is a Trinidadian living in Barbados. She is an example of a Social Entrepreneur. She created and hosts a television program "My Child and I" which is shown in twelve countries across the region via the regional TV station CMC. The programs cover a wide range of parent and child issues such as: Peer Pressure, Bullying, Child Neglect; Parenting on the World Wide Web; Single Parenting; Discipline and more.

Francine recently set up a registered charity, of the same name, which is focused on supporting and initiating a range of effective parenting education projects in Barbados and across the English-speaking Caribbean for the over-all social improvement and well-being of Caribbean families.

http://www.mychild-andi.com/
https://www.facebook.com/mychildandi

Lifestyle Entrepreneur

Claire Worme

Claire Worme is a lifestyle entrepreneur. She started her business, Dingolay in Barbados, in 1992 in her garage. She and her partner, at the time, began by manufacturing exercise wear to take advantage of the opportunity that was provided by the existing aerobics craze. From there they expanded to cotton Lycra casual wear. The company started exporting to the Caribbean, Miami, England and Sweden and soon opened their first retail operation.

An influx of cheap imports made manufacturing not viable and she closed the manufacturing facility around 2006/2007. The company is now strictly retail, but Claire is considering getting back in to a small locally produced collection(s).

When asked why she started the business Claire said that she wanted to be her own boss, have flexible working hours and to be with her family on her terms.

https://www.facebook.com/DingolayBIM

Activity: Use the Internet to find some of the other types of entrepreneurs and read about them. Consider what type of entrepreneur you would like to be.

Chapter 2

• • •

Closed for Stocktaking

Research carried out by Professor Stuart Read of IMB Business School in Switzerland identified some trends in the way expert entrepreneurs managed their businesses in times of uncertainty. The first thing they did before undertaking a new business venture was to assess their means or, put another way, to take stock. This is something that new entrepreneurs can learn from.

He found that they made decisions and took actions based on what they had available by asking the questions:

- Who am I?
- What do I know?
- Who do I know?

Stocktaking will help you to come up with possible businesses that you can start. Let me give you an example of what I mean.

Shanna Belle is a young lady who is very into fashion, make-up and hairstyles and she is interested in starting an online boutique, not just displaying clothes for sale but with a feature to allow shoppers to put outfits together to see how they look before they buy.

This is what her stocktaking might look like.

Who am I?

The hottest fashionista in town.
A diva of fashion.
A master of the makeover (face, hair and clothes)

What do I know?

How to put clothes together and to accessorize outfits
How to apply make up
How to use hairstyles as an accessory
Where to source unique designer clothes
Facebook, Instagram, Twitter

Who do I know?

My brother - web designer
His friend – game designer
Suppliers I have bought unusual clothes from
Over 2000 friends on FB and followers on Instagram and Twitter
Fashion designers from school and other countries (through the Young Fashion Designers' Association)

Do the same exercise for yourself.

Also give some thought to the following questions which may also help you come up with a business idea.

What am I passionate about?

What is lacking in the market i.e. what can't people get?

What do I hear people complaining about?

Based on the answers to those questions, are there any business ideas that come to mind? If not don't despair. Let us look at other options.

Franchises

A Franchise is another option to get into business.

Some entrepreneurs do not necessarily come up with their own business ideas but prefer to take the financial risk of buying and operating a franchise.

The International Franchise Association defines a franchise as:

The agreement or license between two legally independent parties which gives:

- a person or group of people (franchisee) the right to market a product or service using the trademark or trade name of another business (franchisor)
- the franchisee the right to market a product or service using the operating methods of the franchisor
- the franchisee the obligation to pay the franchisor fees for these rights
- the franchisor the obligation to provide rights and support to franchisees

In case you didn't get that, it's where a business or person who has created a product or service (known as the franchisor e.g. Burger King, Subway, KFC) agrees to sell the right to market the product or service (hamburgers, chicken, sandwiches etc.) using their name (Burger King, Macdonald's, Fridays) and the way they operate, to another business or person (the franchisee - entrepreneur) who has to pay them to use the name and the way they operate the business.

So if you go into a Subway franchise anywhere in the world you would have a choice of bread first, then you would choose your meats and cheese, then your toppings and then your sauce before you go to the cashier. That's the way Subway operates. You should never be able to go in and pay first and then choose your bread, meats and toppings.

Franchises are useful where you want to operate a business without having to create your own brand and your own products or service or develop the way you operate the business. However, franchises may require significant investment, depending on the set up.

Activity: Consider whether you would prefer to start your own business or purchase a franchise. Write down the pros and cons of each.

Chapter 3

● ● ●

Market Research

If you decide to start your own business rather than buy a franchise, you need to do some market research. In fact, even if you decide on a franchise you will still need to do research to determine if there is a market for that particular franchise in your area or country.

Market research is the process of collecting valuable information to help you find out if there is a market for your proposed product or service. In other words, if people want or need your product or service and what they will be prepared to pay for it.

Primary Research

Primary research is where you collect information first-hand yourself by using questionnaires to gather data from your potential customers. It can also be done by conducting **focus groups**. (Google *focus groups*)

There are numerous websites which can help you to create a questionnaire to test your business idea. Just Google 'Simple marketing questionnaire' or 'Sample marketing questionnaire'.

They will also help you to understand the various techniques in designing questionnaires such as closed (yes or no) questions, open-ended (require a written answer) questions, multiple choice questions or scaled questions (1-5) to get the information you need to determine if there are people who will buy your product or service and what they think about your existing competition.

Secondary Research

Secondary research is where you access and analyse information that has been collected by someone else such as reports, information on websites, statistics etc. Secondary research is very useful is allowing you to decide on the market you want to target since it can provide information on ages of people, what they spend their money on, the size of the industry you will be getting into, and whether it is an *emerging, rapid growth, mature* or *declining* industry. I will explain these terms below.

Emerging – These are industries in which new products are being developed or patented. These industries generally have no established markets or customer base since they are in the developmental stage. Examples of technologies or products in these industries are holographic projection technology and 3D televisions. If you have not heard of these, that is because they are not widely available on the market as yet.

Rapid growth – Industries in which products or services have passed the innovation stage and demand in the market begins to increase leading to rapid growth. New companies begin to enter the market and compete for market share. Examples would be the mobile device market and the app market.

Mature – Industries in which the product has become established and growth has stabilized. Companies are concerned with maintaining their market share. Examples of these industries would be the automobile and insurance industries.

Declining – As the name suggests, these are industries which have become obsolete. Sales and profits decrease as new innovations enter the market, replacing the existing products or technology. Examples of products in these industries would be the VCR and the camera (film).

Examples of Secondary Market Research

Womenswear: Global Industry Guide
Womenswear: World Market Overview (Market size, Segmentation and Trends Analysis)

Highlights

The global womenswear market grew by 2.6% in 2011 to reach a value of $600,491.7 million.

In 2016, the global womenswear market is forecast to have a value of $662,247.9 million, an increase of 10.3% since 2011.

Europe accounts for 36.8% of the global womenswear market value.

Mobile Industry Statistics

>> Worldwide mobile payment transactions were valued at US$392 billion in 2014 and are expected to reach US $2,849 billion by 2020. (Source: Future Market Insights, 2015)

>> 64% of smartphone owners are now using their mobile devices to shop online (Source: eDigitalResearch and Portaltech Reply, 2012)

>> On Cyber Monday, 10.8% of people used a mobile device to visit a retailer's site, up from 3.9% in 2010. Additionally, mobile sales grew dramatically,

reaching 6.6% on Cyber Monday versus 2.3% in 2010 (Source: IBM's fourth annual Cyber Monday Benchmark, 2011)

>> 74 million consumers in the United States already shop from their mobile devices (Source: InMobi study, 2011)

Chapter 4

• • •

The Journey of a Thousand Miles

The Business Plan

A business plan is a document that describes your business and helps you to:

- clarify your business idea
- spot potential problems
- set out your goals
- measure your progress

It also gives lenders and investors information about the company so that they can make an informed decision about whether the company is likely to be successful and therefore able to repay a loan or give a reasonable return on investment.

Most business plans contain the following sections:

- Executive Summary
- Company Description
- Products & Services
- Marketing Plan

- Operational Plan
- Management & Organization
- Financial Information
- Appendices

Although the executive summary comes first in the plan, it should be written last. The executive summary, as the name suggests, should summarize the contents of the plan in about one or two pages. It's like the beginning of a book; if it doesn't grab your interest the rest won't get read. So, the Executive Summary has got to catch the attention of the reader.

It should contain the following:

- a brief description of the company
- why you believe it will succeed
- your competencies (i.e. what abilities you have) and the competencies of your management team (if you have one)
- the market you will be entering
- how you will operate your business and from where
- the financial requirements including a summary of your estimated revenues and expenses.

Example of an Executive Summary

Divalicious was incorporated in January 2015 and will be operated as an online business which will provide not only exciting and distinctly different clothes for the fashionista (person devoted to fashion clothing, particularly unique or high fashion) but will also allow shoppers to put outfits together virtually with suggestions from a virtual assistant. This will be done using gaming technology. The company will be the first of its kind on the Internet and will have the advantage of being first to market.

Divalicious will sell unique clothing designed by young, audacious designers for young, adventurous women and will be made available via our website for shoppers to put together virtually and purchase online. Presently, our concept is in the introductory stage and is expected to grow rapidly. Our future plans include developing styles for older women in three to four years.

We define our market as teen and young women's casual apparel. The total market size for women's clothing was over $600 billion last year and is expected to grow by 10% this year. We believe we can achieve $1 million in sales within the first two years of operating.

There are a number of sites which offer clothing that can be put together online but none uses game technology or provides a virtual assistant who will offer suggestions to the shopper. In addition, the sites we have investigated are not that easy to navigate. So, while we will be competing with other online clothing stores, we do not consider that we have any competition in the area of the added value that we will be providing by allowing shoppers to create outfits and accessories online and to have advice if they are unsure of what will work.

The management team will be led by the Chief Executive Officer, Shanna Belle, who founded the company in 2015 after graduating with a degree in Fashion Design. She won awards at her college for best portfolio in her year and has held numerous fashion shows. Her team will include Jennifer Nelson, a member of the International Designers Guild, who will source designers for the site, and Patricia White who will be responsible for marketing the business. They will work with photographers, web and gaming designers to create the site.

The facilities of the company will be primarily virtual but *Divalicious* will have a small office located in the Mansion Hill area. The company does not plan to hold stock and will sell clothes on behalf of the designers who will create the clothing and make it available for the site.

The company is seeking $100,000 which will be used to create a high end website, pay for the software to be developed and promote the site globally.

This investment is expected to be repaid within two years out of cash flow. The business is starting with an injection of $10,000 from the owner's parents.

Activity: Look on the Internet for examples of business plans in a business that you are interested in and see what information is presented in the plan.

Chapter 5

• • •

More Steps

The Business Plan Sections

Company Description

This section should include a description of the business and its current operating status, i.e. start-up, developing or expansion; the legal form of the business (sole proprietorship, partnership or incorporated company); the date it was incorporated, if applicable; the major shareholders/partners; and the primary factors which will lead to the success of the business e.g. innovative approaches to service delivery, outstanding customer service etc.

You should also describe the industry in which the company will operate or already operates; its current state and future outlook. If you can access the information, include the size of the industry in terms of revenue earned, persons employed and other relevant information.

The mission of the business and the business philosophy (what is important to you) as well as the goals and objectives should be included in this section.

Goals can be non-specific, subjective and soft in nature, based on your desires for the business.

Objectives must be written in objective language and should follow the SMART rules which are:

Specific
Measurable
Attainable
Realistic
Timely

Products & Services

This is where you can describe in detail your product or service. Areas covered should include the research you have done to test the market (i.e. see if your product/service will sell) and the features and the benefits of the product or service that could give you a competitive position in the market place.

You should also mention future development plans for your product or service.

Drawings, photos, sales brochures, and other bulky items can go in the Appendices section.

Marketing Plan

This section is very important because it provides the evidence to a lender or investor that your product or service will meet the specific needs of customers. In this section, you should indicate who your target market will be; that is, who you are targeting to be your customers, where they are located (if relevant) and what their needs are. If you are able to do so, you should also give an estimate of the size of your market in terms of the type of customers.

Market research provides the basis on which your expectations for your product/service are built. You should indicate who carried out the research, when it was conducted, what method was used (e.g. survey, interviews, questionnaires), the number of participants, conclusions drawn (their reactions to your product or service and how much they are willing to pay for it) and implications. Detailed analyses should be included in the appendices.

Lenders and investors will also want to know something about your competitors - who are the main ones, how long they have been in the business and what you will do to distinguish yourself from them.

Marketing Strategy

This section is very important because it shows the readers of your plan how you intend to meet the sales and margins you projected in the financial statements. This section describes the methods the company plans to use to reach customers and generate sales of its products and services.

You need to provide an overview of:

- The marketing strategy; that is, how you will get yourself known in the market (e.g. by your sales force, advertising, promotions, trade shows, distribution, customer service)
- The company's marketing (positioning) message; that is, how are you selling the product or service (e.g. lowest price, best quality, best service.)
- The company's specific measurable marketing objective - creating company or brand name awareness like Coca Cola; securing a sales presence through a sales force, retail or distribution; achieving market share, unit sales volume, sales price levels, sales revenues.

You should also go into some detail of:

- the sales strategy (size of sales force, training, costs, objectives);
- the advertising/promotion strategy (programs, media to be used, money to be spent, specific advertising & promotion plans);
- distribution/delivery (how the company will distribute or deliver its product, if it will use an outside company); and

- customer service (what service and or support is given, customer service representatives)

Operational Plan

The section on operations should describe the nuts and bolts of the business. If it is a manufacturing business, you should include where the product will be manufactured, the plant, equipment and labour required. If it is a service business, details of how the service will be delivered, if you will require any other skills and where you will source them should be provided. If you are operating a franchise you will need to explain the costs and requirements of the franchise.

A list of your major suppliers and possibly their terms should also be included here.

You may also need to include details of any legal requirements you may have such as permits, health certificates, licenses, trademarks, copyrights, patents etc.

Management & Organization

The purpose of this section is to provide information that demonstrates the qualifications and experience of the management to lead the company. Detailed résumés of all key personnel should be appended.

The name, position and job description of each manager should be included in this section together with a description of their experience and what they bring to the company.

A management organization chart (if applicable) should also be included. This would be for a more established company. Usually, in a start-up situation, there is just the owner and maybe one or two other people who do everything. As the business becomes more sophisticated, specialist managers are hired.

Financial Information

This section is fairly self-explanatory. In it you describe the type of funds you are seeking (debt or equity), how you will use the funds i.e. for capital expenditure, working capital or, in the case, to refinance debt.

You then need to prepare financial projections which should include, at a minimum, an income statement and a balance sheet for three years (sometimes five or even ten year projections may be requested). A cash flow statement should also be included. In a start-up business, an opening balance sheet is required.

Accompanying these statements must be a list of assumptions, otherwise they will be meaningless. The assumptions allow the lender or investor to know the basis on which you have come up with the figures in the projections. So, if you have projected sales of $200,000 per year, your assumptions should say how you came up with that figure so that the reader will know that it wasn't the first number out of a hat. Assumptions should correspond with each line in the income statement and balance sheet.

The financial projections should be prepared by an accountant based on input from you.

Appendices

You should append all relevant documents to your plan. These may include copies of the CVs of the management team, market research material, copies of brochures, copies of contracts and agreements and anything else that you feel will add to your plan.

Activity: Begin to prepare a business plan for your idea.

Chapter 6

• • •

Legal Form - Pros and Cons

There are various forms in which you can set up a business and a number of pros and cons for each form. This chapter outlines each from of the business.

Sole Proprietorship

This is the form of business that is owned by one person. With a sole proprietorship there is no distinction between the entrepreneur and the business from a legal and tax point of view. In other words, the income of the business is considered to be the income of the proprietor for income tax purposes, the assets of the business are owned by the proprietor and liabilities of the business are owed by him/her.

Partnership

Partnerships have many of the same features as sole proprietorships except that they are owned by two or more persons. Assets and liabilities are shared by the partners and income (or losses) from the business is split between partners according to the money each put into the business or according to the partnership agreement. Limited liability partnerships are partnerships in which the liability of some partners is limited to an agreed amount.

Limited Liability Corporation

A limited liability company or corporation is considered to be separate from the owner or owners, who are called shareholders. The main benefit of this type of business structure is the fact that owners are not personally liable for the debts of the company. However, lenders generally ask owners to give personal guarantees for their business loans.

Issue	Sole Proprietorship	Partnership	Corporation
Simplicity	Simplest and least expensive form to establish and maintain	Relatively simple to establish and maintain. A written partnership agreement should be drawn up at the start.	Generally requires the most formality in establishing and maintaining.
Cost	Cheap to file a business name	Cheap to file a business name plus legal fees to prepare the Partnership Agreement.	Cheap to register the company name but more expensive to incorporate the company plus legal fees.
Control	Total control by owner	Shared control by partners	Either total control or shared depending on shareholding
Tax	Individual rates of tax applies	Individual rates of tax on each partner	Corporation tax on net profit
Liability	Unlimited personal liability	Each partner has unlimited personal liability unless it is a limited liability partnership	Liability limited to the amount of paid up share capital unless a personal guarantee is given to cover assets

Chapter 7

• • •

In the Trenches

In the story, Tessa created a questionnaire and carried out a survey to find out what her potential customers thought about her business idea. This is called primary market research.

Activity:

Come up with a business idea for a product or service and test whether it is viable by carrying out market research online.

Google "survey websites" and select one with a free trial. I like SurveyMonkey so I will use that to walk you through the process.

Let's use Tessa's idea of T-shirts with motivational messages to create a brief survey to find out what people think of her idea and whether it will make a feasible business.

1. Go to www.surveymonkey.com
2. Click on Sign up FREE
3. Create a user name and password or sign up using your Facebook or Google account
4. Click on Create Survey
5. Choose Build a new survey from scratch

6. Give your survey a title and choose Market Research
7. Go into Builder and select the type of questionnaire you want to create.

Tessa chooses multiple-choice so her first question may say: Which type of T-shirt do you prefer to wear to campus?

The choices may be

- Plain
- Brand name
- T-shirt with positive message

The next question may be a matrix/rating scale so the questions could be:

Good quality T-shirts are easy to find here
I buy T-shirts often
I would buy a T-shirt with a positive message over any other
Then to find out how much they would be prepared to pay she may choose to use multiple choice again and giver some price ranges for each answer e.g. $20 – 30, $31- 40 etc.

8. When you have completed creating your survey save it and then click on 'Next' at the top of the page. Then copy the web link which you will paste into an e-mail to send to your friends asking them to complete the survey.

The subject could say: I need your feedback

The e-mail could say:

Hi Friend

I'm conducting a very short survey to carry out market research for a business idea I have. I really value your opinion and I'd be glad if you would take two minutes to complete my survey.

Click on the link [Paste link from survey here] to complete the survey.

Thanks for your feedback.

[Your name]

Send the e-mail to all your contacts. As they respond, SurveyMonkey will compile the information for you and give you the results so that you can see how people respond to your questions and, therefore, if your business idea looks like it might be viable.

Play around with different types of answer options but don't make your survey too long or people may not complete it.

Have fun!

Chapter 8

• • •

Starting Over

In the story, Tessa had to start over after her market research revealed that her business would not be viable. While students were interested in T-shirts with positive messages, the majority was only prepared to pay between 30 – 40 dollars and, after researching the costs to get the T-shirts ready for sale, Tessa realized that the duties and tariffs on her imported T-shirts pushed the price beyond what her market was prepared to pay.

So, what are tariffs and duties?

Duties and tariffs are taxes that have to be paid to the government on imported goods. The two words can sometimes be used interchangeably, but occasionally only one is correct. For example:

"How much duty did you have to pay on the T-shirts?"

"The Minister of Finance commented on the effect of tariffs on the economy."

As these examples show, when we refer to the system of government-imposed duties or the list of those duties, the word 'tariff' is more appropriate, but the word 'duty' or 'customs duty' is more appropriate when we're talking about specific amounts.

The tariff or duty is charged on the value of the goods imported, including freight and insurance.

Some countries have high duties on imported goods and others have low duties. When countries have trade agreements, the duties are usually lower as they have preferential rates of duty but this is becoming less common.

Governments tend to impose duties or tariffs on goods imported into the country in order to protect their local industries. In Tessa's case, T-shirts were made in her country, although she did not like the quality, so in order to protect the businesses that made T-shirts, the government charged high duties on imported T-shirts so that competing products brought into the country would cost a lot more and consumers would be less likely to buy them and would, therefore, support the local businesses.

Imposing high duties on imported items is also designed to reduce the desire for these items by making them more expensive and therefore saving the foreign exchange which would be necessary to buy the goods from foreign countries.

Duties and tariffs also raise revenue for governments. The more items businesses import and have to pay duties on, the more money they have to pay over to the Government.

Although governments earn revenue on imports, they prefer businesses to export goods rather than import since exports bring in money from other countries and boost foreign reserves.

Activity: If you are already thinking about a business, research what the duties are on any material you may need to import.

Chapter 9

• • •

In the Trenches...Again

In Chapter 8 of Tessa's Story, Tessa realized that her business idea was not viable and she had to come up with another idea and do more research to see if that one would be viable. It was a hard lesson for her to learn but that is all part of business. Fortunately for her, she did not get as far as starting the business so the lesson she learned was relatively painless.

Many successful entrepreneurs do not succeed in their first business venture and many experience business failures even after operating successful businesses. The important lesson they share is to persevere and never give up.

Here are two examples of entrepreneurs who have experienced business failures, one international and one regional.

Walt Disney

Walt Disney is proof that your beginning does not have to be your end. He ran away from home while still fairly young. He was fired from his first job for lacking creativity and went bankrupt at age 22 when his first company failed. He had several more business failures, but wouldn't give up on his dream to succeed as an animator. His first success came with the animation of Snow White after which he had many successes and some failures along the way but he has left a legacy. Today we still watch Disney cartoons and Disney Land is visited by millions of people every year.

Ralph "Bizzy" Williams

Ralph Williams, known in the business community as "Bizzy", is a successful Barbadian entrepreneur. He is the Founder and Chairman of Williams Industries Inc. which is a group of eighteen companies. In 2001 he won the Ernst & Young World Entrepreneur of the Year Award for Multiple Business Creation in Monte Carlo from participants drawn from countries worldwide. In spite of his business successes he experienced a major business failure a few years ago when Red Jet, an airline in which he was a major investor, folded. He admits that it was his worst business failure to date, however that has not deterred him from investing in other business ventures.

The Business Model Canvas

Joshua also suggested that Tessa prepare a Business Model Canvas to paint a picture of the way she plans to operate her business.

Activity: Go to www.strategyzer.com and download a template of the Business Canvas Model and complete it for your business or business idea.

The Business Model Canvas

Key Partners	Key Activities	Value Propositions	Customer Relationships	Customer Segments
Who are your key partners/suppliers? Which key resources are you getting from your partners? What key activities do partners perform	What key activities does your value proposition require? What are the key activities in your distribution channels, your customer relationships, in generating revenue stream?	What value do you deliver to the customer? Which of your customer's problems are you helping to solve? Which needs are you meeting?	What type of relationships will you have with your customers? For example, personal assistance, self-service, automated system. How can you integrate that into your business in terms of cost and format?	Who are you creating value for? Who is your most important customer? Example: mass market, niche market, diversified.
	Key Resources What key resources does your value proposition require? What resources are most important in distribution channels, customer relationships, and revenue stream? Intellectual (patents, copyrights, data), physical resources, human resources, financial resources.		**Channels** Through which channels do your customers want to be reached? Which channels work best? How much do they cost? How can they be integrated into your and your customers' routines?	

Cost Structure	Revenue streams
What are the most important costs inherent in your business model? Which key resources/ activities are most expensive?	For what value are your customers willing to pay? What are they currently paying for?

www.strategyzer.com

Chapter 10

• • •

Financing the Business

The major cause of failure in start-up businesses is lack of money. Money is needed to buy fixed assets such as vehicles, equipment and furniture, which are used in the business to generate revenue. It is also needed for operating or working capital to run the business, i.e. to buy raw material or stock and to pay expenses.

Sources of Capital

There are two main sources of capital in a business: debt and equity.

Equity

Equity is money invested in the business as capital or, as the business progresses, money retained by the business called retained earnings. Sometimes an entrepreneur may ask family and friends to invest in the business or possibly a wealthy person (known as an Angel Investor) may consider the business a worthwhile investment and offer to invest in it. Another source of equity finance is from Venture Capital Funds (VCF).

VCFs are companies set up and financed by the pooling of funds from large organizations such as insurance companies, corporations, banks and even wealthy individuals. These funds will usually provide equity to a company which:

- has a high growth potential
- is well managed with reputable owners/managers
- can provide a high return on the investment
- can generate a return in 4-7 years.

Debt

Debt is another source of capital. Start-up companies, however, should try to avoid debt as much as possible since the interest payments can be a burden on the business and in most cases bank and financial institutions generally will not lend to start-up companies. Loans can be raised from friends and family or by using credit card debt.

Bank debt is either by way of a credit facility (overdraft) or a term loan. An overdraft facility is generally used to fund working capital and is, therefore, short term in nature. The facility is reviewed annually and interest is charged on the balance outstanding so that the interest you pay varies according to your use of the facility.

A term loan, on the other hand, is a loan made for a specific time, usually from three to seven years, but could be longer or shorter. The interest rate is generally fixed at the time of the loan but provision may be made for it to be reviewed during the life of the loan. In both cases, the bank will require security for their loan - either what is called a charge over the fixed assets or over the floating assets or both. Floating assets are items like stock, accounts receivable and short-term investments.

Other Sources of Finance

Suppliers can be an informal source of short-term finance. If your supplier gives you 30 or 60 days to settle your account, you are in essence being "loaned" that money. You, therefore, have use of that money for 30 or 60 days for other activities, provided that you can pay your bill when it becomes due. Failure to pay bills when they fall due will quickly remove the privilege of receiving credit.

A more recent source of finance is crowdfunding. Crowdfunding is the collection of finance from backers—the "crowd"—to fund a business or an initiative and usually occurs on Internet platforms. There are three types of crowdfunding:

1. Equity Based Crowdfunding: Investors receive a stake in the company.
2. Lending Based Crowdfunding: Investors are repaid for their investment over a period of time.
3. Reward Based Crowdfunding: Investors receive a tangible item or service in return for their funds.

A Word on Borrowing

While this chapter provides information on how to source finance, this does not mean that debt should be your first option. When you borrow, you are no longer a free agent to do as you like with your business. You have to report your company's performance to the lender, you cannot sell assets if they are pledged as security and you have to inform the lender of any major changes you are contemplating in the business.

Activity: Consider the pros and cons of the different type of financing mentioned above.

Chapter 11

• • •

Protect Your Property

Today knowledge based economies are becoming more prevalent. Many of the products and services we use today are the fruit of someone's knowledge. That knowledge needs to be protected so that other people cannot replicate it or use it without permission.

According to the World Intellectual Property Organization, Intellectual Property (IP) refers to creations of the mind, such as inventions; literary and artistic works; designs; and symbols, names and images used in commerce.[5]

The different types of intellectual property include:

Copyright

Copyright is a legal term used to describe the rights that creators have over their literary and artistic works. Works covered by copyright range from books, music, paintings, sculpture and films, to computer programs, databases, advertisements, maps and technical drawings. Copyright is depicted by the symbol ©.

When people copy music or movies illegally and sell it without the artist getting the benefit, they are infringing on the artist's copyright and can be subject to fines.

Patents

A patent is an exclusive right granted for an invention. Generally speaking, a patent provides the patent owner with the right to decide how - or whether - the invention can be used by others. In exchange for this right, the patent owner makes technical information about the invention publicly available in the published patent document.

Trademarks

A trademark is a sign capable of distinguishing the goods or services of one enterprise from those of other enterprises. Trademarks date back to ancient times when craftsmen used to put their signature or "mark" on their products. Trademarks are denoted by ™.

A trademark identifies a word, name, sound, symbol or colour that distinguishes a good or service used in commerce. In the story, Tessa decided to call her magazine *Caribelle* and she was advised to trademark the name so that no-one could use it.

Industrial Designs

An industrial design constitutes the ornamental or aesthetic aspect of an article. A design may consist of three-dimensional features, such as the shape or surface of an article, or of two-dimensional features, such as patterns, lines or colour.

Note: The processes to copyright, register a trademark, patent or industrial design vary from country to country so you need to research how it is done in your country if you have a business where you have intellectual property.

Activity: If your product is knowledge based, consider what type of intellectual property protection you should employ.

Consider ways in which you may have knowingly or unknowingly infringed on someone's intellectual property. How has it disadvantaged them? How would you feel if someone did it to you?

Chapter 12

• • •

A Contract? You're joking!

In Chapter 12 of Tessa's story, Joshua presented Tessa with a contract to sign when he agreed to invest US$5,000 in her business. Tessa was a bit put out because she felt that Joshua did not trust her but he told her that she should get into the habit of using contracts in business. Contracts are legally binding and can save a lot of problems in the long run if the relationship changes or if someone does not live up to their agreement.

Contracts

One of the best definitions of a contract I have come across is from www. freeadvice.com. It says:

A contract is an agreement between two or more persons (individuals, businesses, organizations, or government agencies) to do, or to refrain from doing, a particular thing in exchange for something of value.

There are all types of contracts. Two of the more common types for entrepreneurs, depending on the business they are involved, may be letters of engagement, rental agreements and employee contracts. There are many free templates available on the Internet.

Letters of Engagement

Letters of engagement tend to be used more by accountants and other professionals such as lawyers, investment bankers etc. An entrepreneur is, therefore, more likely to be the one receiving the engagement letter than giving it.

Rental Agreements

A rental agreement can be used to describe a lease in which the asset is tangible property like land, a house, an office space or a car. Rental agreements cover the use of the asset, the cost of renting the asset, the obligations of the landlord and the tenant as well as the term of the rental.

Employee Contracts

Employee contracts are contracts given by the employer to the employee at the beginning of employment. It should include the start date of the job, job title, the roles and responsibilities of the employee, the remuneration, entitlement for holidays, sick leave, maternity or paternity leave, work hours and various other aspects of the employment.

Activity: Based on your business venture, what kind of contracts do you think you might need? Look on the Internet for examples of different types of contracts.

Chapter 13

• • •

Another Entrepreneurial Venture

In the related chapter of the story, Tessa's magazine features *Savon Naturel,* a business started by Candace Balmain, an entrepreneur in Dominica. Since she is also running a business, she has some similar issues to deal with such as suppliers, but because she creates tangible products she has additional issues such as location and materials to deal with. We will look at these briefly.

Suppliers

Suppliers provide goods and services to businesses and therefore businesses rely on them to either create their products or offer their services. In the story Tessa's suppliers provided articles and photos for her magazine whereas Candace's suppliers provided raw materials for her to make her soaps.

Materials

Materials are the supplies needed to make a product. In the case of *Savon Naturel,* the materials include coconut oil, shea butter, shredded coconut, noni seeds, aloe and other ingredients. The materials were all locally sourced, apart from the shea butter which had to be imported.

Entrepreneurs need high quality materials to manufacture their products and also a reliable source of those materials so that production and, therefore, supply of goods, is not affected by shortage of materials needed to create the product.

If materials have to be imported to create the product, entrepreneurs should investigate various sources and also find out about the duties that these imports may be subject to before they purchase them from overseas suppliers.

Location

Depending on the type of business, location can be very important to the entrepreneur. For a retail business, where customers are coming into the business, you know the important rule: location, location, location.

The location:

- Should be selected based on your target market – If you are catering to a niche market and your customers will literally travel to the ends of the earth to get to you, then your location is not a big concern. However, if you are catering to customers who travel by public transportation, then you need to be located near to bus stops. If your customers are drivers, you need to have adequate parking.
- Must be visible and well identified with signage – This is fairly obvious because you want your customers to be able to find you. If you also rely on passing traffic, then your sign needs to attract their attention.
- Must be comfortable for your customers – Your customers must be comfortable to come to and receive service at your business place. If they feel unsafe or uncomfortable, they will quickly find somewhere else where they feel more at ease.

In choosing a location for your business you should also do some preliminary research to find out the history of the location, that is, what type of businesses occupied the space, why they move out, if they were similar businesses to yours etc.

Before signing a lease or a rental agreement you should check out the rents that other tenants are paying as well as do some basic research into rents charged in other areas of similar standard. You also need to find out who will be responsible for leasehold improvements (you or your landlord) and if there are any restrictions on what he/she will allow.

In the case of Candace Balmain, she operated out of her home until her business began to grow and then she needed to move to a proper manufacturing facility. This meant that she would then have to enter a rental agreement, pay rent and ensure that her suppliers could easily get to her. Since she did not have a shop front, the concerns with customers finding her would not have been great. However, if she decided to retail her soaps she would need to consider the issues outlined above.

Activity: Based on the type of business you are contemplating or are already operating, what are some of the issues you are facing? What are you doing or what will you do to deal with them?

Chapter 14

• • •

Growing the Business

As a business begins to grow, the owner will need to take on staff to deal with different aspects of the business. Eventually it may even have departments to deal with the specialized areas and these relationships between positions and departments can be represented diagrammatically in an organization chart.

What is an Organization Chart?

An organizational chart is a diagram that shows the management structure of an organization, showing the responsibilities of each department, the relationships of the departments to each other and the lines of authority and responsibility in the organization.

The Organization Chart for Joshua's Business

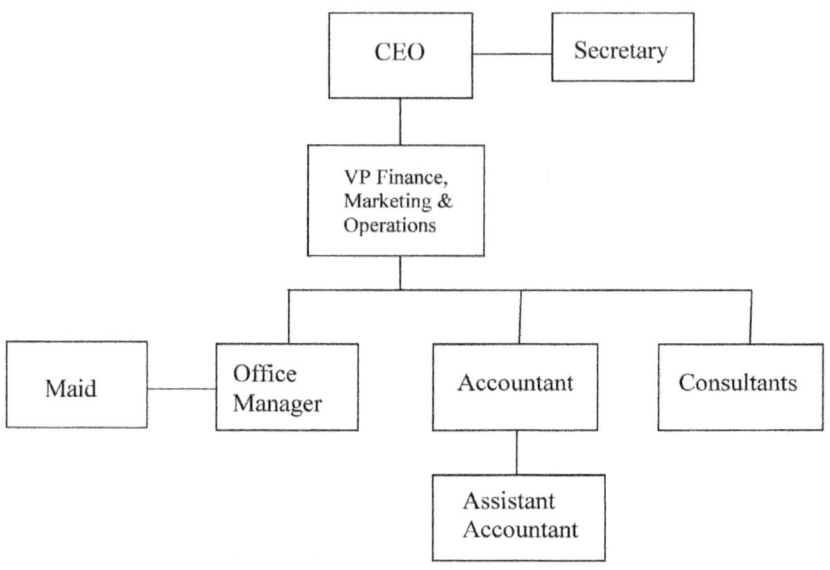

As CEO, Joshua is the leader of his business.

What is Leadership?

Here are the definitions of leadership from some well-known business leaders.

Peter Drucker: "The only definition of a leader is someone who has followers."

Warren Bennis: "Leadership is the capacity to translate vision into reality."

Bill Gates: "As we look ahead into the next century, leaders will be those who empower others."

John Maxwell: "Leadership is influence – nothing more, nothing less."

The Six Leadership Styles (Goleman)

	Coercive	Authoritative	Affiliative	Democratic	Pacesetting	Coaching
The Leader's modus operandi	Demands immediate compliance	Mobilizes people toward a vision	Creates harmony and builds emotional bonds	Forges consensus through participation	Sets high standards for performance	Develops people for the future
The style in a phrase	"Do what I tell you"	"Come with me"	"People come first"	"What do you think?"	"Do as I do"	"Try this"
Underlying emotional intelligence competencies	Drive to achieve, initiative, self-control	Self-confidence, empathy, change catalyst	Empathy, building relationships, communication	Collaboration, team leadership, communi-cation	Conscientious-ness, drive to achieve, initiative	Developing others, empathy, self-awareness
When the style works best	In a crisis to kick start a turnaround, or with problem employees	When changes require a new vision or when a clear direction is needed	To heal rifts in a team or to motivate people during stressful circumstances	To build buy-in or consensus, or get input from valuable employees	To get quick results from a highly motivated team	To help an employee improve performance or develop long-term strengths
Overall impact on climate	Negative	Most strongly positive	Positive	Positive	Negative	Positive

Goleman, Daniel, "Leadership that Gets Results"
Harvard Business Review. March –April 2000
p.82-83

https://hbr.org/2000/03/leadership-that gets-results

Chapter 15

• • •

What is the Purpose of this Business?

Joshua and his team went on a retreat to so strategic planning for his business. Before they got into the actual planning, he went over the mission and vision of the business which helped them to determine what strategies they needed to employ to achieve the vision.

The Mission

The mission defines the purpose of the business, i.e. why it was started, to offer what kind of service and to which customers. Some mission statements include all of these issues and some do not. It is a matter of choice as to what you put in it. What is important is that you identify the purpose of the business.

Example

An entrepreneur is setting up a boutique.

The following have been established:

> The product is high quality business wear and accessories.
> The customer is the professional woman.

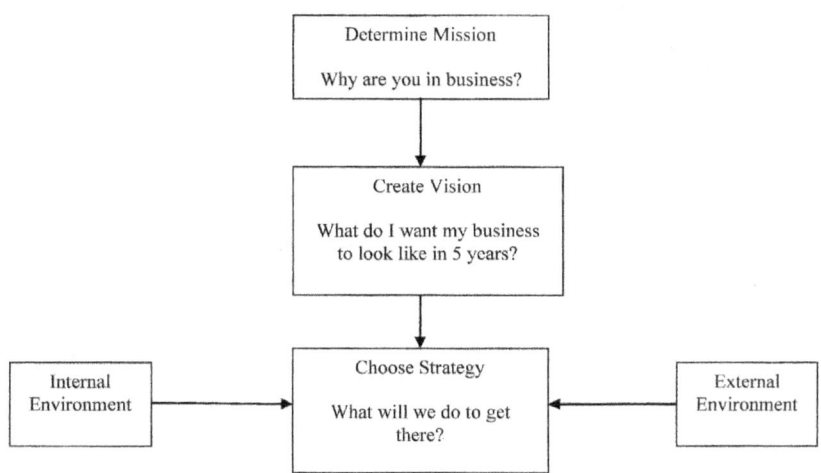

The distinguishing features of the business are: a store totally dedicated to providing business wear; a large selection of clothes; high quality apparel; reasonable prices; and excellent service.

Clothes will be imported or the manufacture of certain items will be outsourced.

The mission of the company is as follows:

> To provide high quality business wear and accessories
> For the professional woman
> And
> Service which makes her
> Feel valued

The Vision

The vision of the business is a mental picture of what the business should look like at a particular point in time. The vision will, therefore, change as time progresses and as the business changes.

When you have no vision the focus of the business is lost. When that happens there is no standard to refer to, so you get caught up in following your competitors and trying to be all things to all people. You essentially deviate from the intended purpose of the business and (unless you also change your strategy) this will lead to failure in the long run.

It is, therefore, imperative that you create a vision for your business. This will become your beacon, your point of reference, so that when your competitors start to do something you can weigh it against your vision and see if it makes sense for your business in light of what you are trying to accomplish.

The vision is derived from the mission.

In this example the vision could be:

> To be the boutique of
> First choice for the
> Professional woman by the year 2020,
> Providing quality business wear
> And service
> Which makes her
> Feel valued.

The vision must be feasible (capable of being achieved in the time frame) and flexible (capable of changing to suit the circumstances).

SWOT Analysis

Before we choose our strategy, it is important to do a SWOT analysis; that is, an analysis of the

Strengths
Weaknesses

Opportunities
Threats

This involves creating a list of the strengths of the business in relation to the vision. That is, what are the strengths that will enable the business to fulfil its vision? For example, a strength could be "Highly skilled seamstresses, specialising in tailored clothes."

What weaknesses does the business have which may hinder its ability to fulfil the vision? A weakness could be "Inability to carry a full range of accessories due to lack of space."

What opportunities are open to the business to enhance its success in achieving the vision? An opportunity could be "Ability to manufacture suits in Trinidad at a lower price and import them into Barbados."

What are the threats that could prevent the vision from being achieved? A threat could be "Developing trend of professional women going overseas to shop rather than buying locally."

In terms of the external environment, we also need to look at political, economic, social and technological (PEST) issues that may impact the businesses either positively or negatively. We need to be aware of these so that we will adopt the appropriate strategies.

Goals

Goals provide the link between the mission and vision and the actual day-to-day operations of the business. They are what the company needs to achieve at the level of the day-to-day running of the business to make the vision a reality.

When setting goals we need to look at what we are trying to achieve according to the vision. In addition, there are other important areas which might not be included in the vision statement but which impact on the business's ability to achieve the vision. These include areas such as employees, financial management, community outreach and technology. There may be others.

From the example, the key points of the vision used to set goals would be:

"…boutique of first choice" (marketing & image focus)
"…quality business wear (product focus)
"…provide service which makes her feel valued" (customer focus)

The goals of this business could, therefore, be:

Marketing & Image: To be recognised as the boutique of first choice for business wear for the professional woman.

Product: To provide business wear and accessories of the highest quality and greatest comfort to our customers.

Customer: To consistently provide a level of service that makes the customer feel valued and which creates customer loyalty.

Other important goals may be:

Staff: To provide a working environment for our staff that motivates them to satisfy our customers.

Financial Management: To ensure that we manage our finances well in order to grow our business and meet the needs of our shareholders and our staff.

Community: To assist the community in which we are located through donations of time and money.

Objectives

Objectives are stepping stones to achieve the goals. They must be specific and measurable.

The objectives to achieve the Marketing & Image goal might be:

To rank as the most recognized and chosen business wear boutique by June, 2019 in an independent survey.

Strategies

Strategies are the methods that are chosen to achieve the objectives.

In order to be considered as the boutique of first choice for business wear, some of the strategies which may be pursued are:

- Hold bi-annual fashion shows for professional women
- Get a column in the press and write about business wear trends for women
- Create a Facebook fan page and build Likes
- Do e-mail blasts to customers telling them of new arrivals etc.
- Always be well stocked

Action Plans

Action plans are the detailed steps that need to be taken to carry out the strategies.

For example if we decide to write a column in one of our local newspapers, the actions plans would be:

- Contact the editor of the newspaper and sell the idea
- Prepare a list of topics you intend to cover

- Write the articles
- Submit them to the newspaper

That is just a brief example of the way each goal would need to be worked through.

While the strategic planning process is carried out in-house by some large companies, and a start-up company could probably pull together its own plan, generally, the most efficient method of carrying out the strategic planning process is to use a consultant to facilitate the process. The use of an external facilitator brings objectivity, focus and discipline to the process.

Activity: What is the purpose of your business? To get to the purpose ask why until you can get no further answer. That is the purpose.

Where do you want your business to be in about three to five years? That is your vision.

BIBLIOGRAPHY

1. www.SBA.gov

2. https://en.wikipedia.org/wiki/Entrepreneurship

3. http://www.startupdonut.co.uk/startup/business-planning/writing-a-business-plan

4. http://thebusinessplanblog.com/%E2%80%9Cgoals%E2%80%9D-and-%E2%80%9Cobjectives%E2%80%9D-know-the-difference-get-better-results/

5. http://www.wipo.int/about-ip/en/index.html

www.ingramcontent.com/pod-product-compliance
Lightning Source LLC
Chambersburg PA
CBHW070231210526
45168CB00020B/1903